VOCABULARY
SUCCESS STAGE III

IVY LEAGUE

Icon English Ivy League Vocabulary Success Stage III

Copyright © 2019 by Icon English Institute

No part of this publication may be reproduced, distributed, or transmitted in any form or by any means, including photocopying, recording, or other electronic or mechanical methods, without the prior written permission of the author, except in the case of brief quotations embodied in critical reviews and certai other non-commercial uses permitted by copyright law.

Icon English
www.iconenglish.com

TABLE OF CONTENTS

Stage Three A

- Lesson One 12
- Lesson Two 14
- Lesson Three 16
- Lesson Four 18
- Lesson Five 20
- Lesson Six 22
- Lesson Seven 24
- Lesson Eight 26
- Lesson Nine 28
- Lesson Ten 30
- Lesson Eleven 32
- Lesson Twelve 34
- Lesson Thirteen 36
- Lesson Fourteen 38
- Lesson Fifteen 40
- Lesson Sixteen 42
- Lesson Seventeen 44
- Lesson Eighteen 46
- Lesson Nineteen 48
- Lesson Twenty 50
- Lesson Twenty one 52
- Lesson Twenty two 54
- Lesson Twenty three 56
- Lesson Twenty four 58
- Lesson Twenty five 60
- Lesson Twenty six 62
- Lesson Twenty seven 64
- Lesson Twenty eight 66
- Lesson Twenty nine 68
- Lesson Thirty 70
- Lesson Thirty one 72
- Lesson Thirty two 74
- Lesson Thirty three 76
- Lesson Thirty four 78
- Lesson Thirty five 80
- Lesson Thirty six 82

TABLE OF CONTENTS

Stage Three A

- Lesson Thirty seven 84
- Lesson Thirty eight 86
- Lesson Thirty nine 88
- Lesson Forty 90
- Lesson Forty one 92
- Lesson Forty two 94
- Lesson Forty three 96
- Lesson Forty four 98
- Lesson Forty five 100
- Lesson Forty six 102
- Lesson Forty seven 104
- Lesson Forty eight 106
- Lesson Forty nine 108
- Lesson Fifty 110

TABLE OF CONTENTS

Stage Three B

- Lesson One 114
- Lesson Two 116
- Lesson Three 118
- Lesson Four 120
- Lesson Five 122
- Lesson Six 124
- Lesson Seven 126
- Lesson Eight 128
- Lesson Nine 130
- Lesson Ten 132
- Lesson Eleven 134
- Lesson Twelve 136
- Lesson Thirteen 138
- Lesson Fourteen 140
- Lesson Fifteen 142
- Lesson Sixteen 144
- Lesson Seventeen 146
- Lesson Eighteen 148
- Lesson Nineteen 150
- Lesson Twenty 152
- Lesson Twenty one 154
- Lesson Twenty two 156
- Lesson Twenty three 158
- Lesson Twenty four 160
- Lesson Twenty five 162
- Lesson Twenty six 164
- Lesson Twenty seven 166
- Lesson Twenty eight 168
- Lesson Twenty nine 170
- Lesson Thirty 172
- Lesson Thirty one 174
- Lesson Thirty two 176
- Lesson Thirty three 178
- Lesson Thirty four 180
- Lesson Thirty five 182
- Lesson Thirty six 184

TABLE OF CONTENTS

Stage Three B

- Lesson Thirty seven 186
- Lesson Thirty eight 188
- Lesson Thirty nine 190
- Lesson Forty 192
- Lesson Forty one 194
- Lesson Forty two 196
- Lesson Forty three 198
- Lesson Forty four 200
- Lesson Forty five 202
- Lesson Forty six 204
- Lesson Forty seven 206
- Lesson Forty eight 208
- Lesson Forty nine 210
- Lesson Fifty 212

INTRODUCTION

Icon English Ivy League Vocabulary Success is a series of books, each of which is intended for you to use when learning English. What's great about our books is that they can be used either with a teacher in a classroom setting or independently in your own time.

Vocabulary is one of the most vital aspects of learning a language. Without a rich vocabulary, how do you express the things you want to say? Furthermore, many students will find that having a vast lexicon can be a huge help when taking exams or writing essays for school. And, though some words may not be used in everyday conversations, less common words are still important to learn for certain assignments or standardized tests. Language is varied and complex. Your vocabulary should be that way too.

To keep things simple, each lesson is comprised of ten words. Their meanings, forms and parts of speech need your full attention so that you can learn how to determine which word in what form works best in which fill-in-the-blank sentence. After the sentences, you will read a passage. These passages contain the same ten words from your vocabulary lesson. Reading these words in a narrative context will help you understand how these words are used, and how you can apply them yourself.

WHO IS THIS SERIES AIMED AT?

STAGE ZERO: BASIC

Stage Zero begins with a "dead word" and a word list. We call words like happy, tired, or pretty "dead" because they are so overused that their meanings fall flat. Included beneath each "dead word" are other, more complicated words with similar meanings. Stage Zero will help you precisely express what you're trying to say without resorting to stale language. Each word list is sorted into categories so that you can really concentrate your language and distinguish yourself for excellent diction whenever you speak or write in English.

STAGE I: INTERMEDIATE

After completing Stage Zero, you will have absorbed many intriguing new words. However, Stage I is different. These lessons are aimed at high school students who want to improve their writing skills. Many high school assignments require students to analyze complicated works of literature, but how can you complete those difficult assignments if you can't comprehend the words being used? Stage I will help you discover new, complicated words that you will come across in your classes. Boost your essay marks by completing Stage I!

STAGE II: ADVANCED

Stage II covers some of the complex words in the English language. Much like Stage I, Stage II will provide you with a word list (plus their part of speech and meaning), fill-in-the-blank sentences, and a short passage. The words in Stage II were chosen by combing through SAT tests from the past few years and picking out the most common words used. However, even if you don't plan on taking the SAT's or ACT's, Stage II is still a vital part of helping you become a fluent speaker and writer of English! Take your skills to the next level and conquer Stage II!

STAGE III: MASTERY

Stage III covers 500 most complex words in the English language. Much like Stage II, Stage III will provide you with a word list (plus their part of speech and meaning), fill-in-the-blank sentences, and a short passage. The words in Stage III were chosen by combing through standardised exams like AP English, ACT, and SAT tests from the past few years and picking out the most challenging words used. However, even if you don't plan on taking any standardised exam like the SAT's or ACT's, Stage III is still a vital part of improving your reading comprehension and enhancing your writing skills!

STAGE
THREE A

LESSON ONE

Target Words

1. Abase
2. Abate
3. Abbreviate
4. Abduct
5. Aberration
6. Abhor
7. Abide
8. Abject
9. Abort
10. Abridge

LESSON ONE

A. Dictation

____/10

B. Fill in the blanks with the most appropriate words

01 The National Aeronautics and Space Administration _____ their name to NASA.

02 A child went missing last week after being _____ from a playground.

03 To say I dislike asparagus is an understatement. I _____ it!

04 The deep sea divers had to _____ their exploration when the oxygen in their tanks started running low.

05 There was a robbery next door, but such criminal activity is an _____ in this area.

06 The employee _____ himself by yelling crude things at his superiors and was promptly fired.

07 Our teacher will not _____ cheating or plagiarism in the classroom.

08 My mom likes to read _____ versions of books because she doesn't have much time to read.

09 The storm suddenly _____, and the sun peeked through the clouds.

10 Bankruptcy plunged him into _____ poverty.

LESSON TWO

Target Words

1. Abrogate
2. Abscond
3. Abundant
4. Accede
5. Accentuate
6. Accommodating
7. Accost
8. Acumen
9. Acute
10. Affable

LESSON TWO

A. Dictation

____/10

B. Fill in the blanks with the most appropriate words

01 This dog has an _____ personality, so it's no wonder he was adopted so quickly!

02 We _____ from the pep rally to hang out in the art room.

03 You must have _____ and patience to be a teacher of any grade or class.

04 My cat has an _____ sense of smell.

05 The president will _____ the healthcare law.

06 A solicitor standing outside the grocery _____ most of the people passing by.

07 The general store has an _____ reserve of party supplies.

08 Her slim-fitting dress _____ her figure.

09 Our babysitter is very _____. She helps us out whenever she can.

10 We will not _____ to the robber's ludicrous demands.

LESSON THREE

Target Words

1. Affluent
2. Aggrandize
3. Aggregate
4. Aghast
5. Agoraphobia
6. Akimbo
7. Alacrity
8. Algid
9. Allay
10. Alleviate

LESSON THREE

A. Dictation

_____ /10

B. Fill in the blanks with the most appropriate words

01 He put ice on the mosquito bite to _____ the itching.

02 I grew up in an _____ neighbourhood with big houses and fancy cars.

03 The president _____ himself by acting like he was a financial and entrepreneurial king.

04 His mean-spirited and brutally honest comments left me utterly _____.

05 The scores were _____, and the championship went to the team with the highest one.

06 Ruth has _____ and cannot go outside due to her condition.

07 The _____ with which the dolphin swam was astonishing.

08 The apartment was _____ and frosty because Claire left the window open all night.

09 She stood _____, staring at me with a confused expression.

10 I _____ the growing tension by asking them to take a deep breath and speak slowly.

LESSON FOUR

Target Words

1. Aloof
2. Altercation
3. Amalgamation
4. Ambivalent
5. Amble
6. Ameliorate
7. Amend
8. Amiable
9. Amourous (US Amorous)
10. Amorphous

LESSON FOUR

A. Dictation

____ /10

B. Fill in the blanks with the most appropriate words

01 We _____ past the old, haunted cemetery and were careful not to walk too close.

02 My mom _____ disputes between my siblings by being fair and hearing both sides.

03 The reviewer was _____ about the movie. He couldn't decide if he loved or hated it!

04 The universe is an _____ thing, unrestricted by time or space.

05 My friend and I had been fighting but we finally made _____.

06 The CEO announced that an _____ with the competing company was under way.

07 My cat's purrs have become quite _____ since I got a female cat to keep him company.

08 The film student was very _____, owing to the fact that she spent so much time watching movies!

09 I had an _____ with the gas station attendant when he tried to overcharge me.

10 The people living next door are not very _____ or considerate.

LESSON FIVE

Target Words

1. Anomaly
2. Antechamber
3. Anxiety
4. Aphorism
5. Apocalypse
6. Apparitional
7. Arbitrator
8. Ascetic
9. Assuage
10. Atone (for)

LESSON FIVE

A. Dictation

____ /10

B. Fill in the blanks with the most appropriate words

01 Though his family is quite boisterous, Roger is a total _____; he is actually very reserved!

02 The movie is about a young girl trying to survive in a desolate world after the _____ strikes.

03 Our professor will act as _____ in today's class debate.

04 He stockpiles clichéd _____ like a squirrel hoards acorns!

05 My _____ about being on large ships only got worse after I watched *Titanic*.

06 The _____ creature hovered over the bed, watching us sleep like a silent shadow.

07 Her upbringing in a Catholic household led to her _____ nature.

08 Billy promised to _____ for breaking the front windows on Miss Caroline's house.

09 The doctor asked his test patients to wait in the _____ while he readied the examination room.

10 The politician attempted to _____ protestors by promising to repeal the unfair law, but the protestors knew he was lying.

LESSON SIX

Target Words

1. Audacious
2. Augment
3. Austere
4. Baleful
5. Bard
6. Battery
7. Belligerent
8. Benevolent
9. Benign
10. Berate

LESSON SIX

A. Dictation

____/10

B. Fill in the blanks with the most appropriate words

01 The giant, angry dog gave me a _____ glare that sent me running home.

02 Kevin is an _____ young man who will not be intimidated by your ridiculous claims.

03 We listened to the _____ recite a poem by William Butler Yeats.

04 Susanna was relieved to hear that the tumour on her lung was _____.

05 Miss Prince is an _____-looking woman with sharp features and high, arching eyebrows.

06 After too many beers, Jonathan was acting _____. He tried to fight the bar security guard!

07 Henry was arrested for _____ after the cops witnessed him punch an innocent bystander.

08 The judge _____ the young delinquents for putting other people in harm's way with their prank.

09 She uses makeup to _____ her eyes.

10 Hagrid is a _____ and good-hearted character in the *Harry Potter* books.

LESSON SEVEN

Target Words

1. Bereft
2. Bide
3. Bilk
4. Blandish
5. Bloated
6. Boisterous
7. Bourgeois
8. Brash
9. Brazen
10. Brumal

LESSON SEVEN

A. Dictation

____ /10

B. Fill in the blanks with the most appropriate words

01 The _____ weather made me want to hide under warm blankets and drink a hot cup of tea.

02 Our _____ neighbourhood is populated with modest houses and middle-class families.

03 I left the ravioli noodles in water too long, and now they are _____ and mushy.

04 The fourth-grade class was hyperactive and _____ during the school Halloween party.

05 He _____ his poker buddies, so they kicked him out of the club for good.

06 The car was _____ of gas. We left it on the side of the highway and walked to the gas station.

07 Wolves will _____ their time until their prey is vulnerable, and then they attack.

08 Henry is a _____ fellow who is unafraid of a challenge.

09 My _____ uncle tells crude jokes at family gatherings, much to the chagrin of my mother.

10 The interviewee _____ his interviewer in an attempt to win his favour.

LESSON EIGHT

Target Words

1. Brusque
2. Buffet
3. Buffet
4. Burgeon
5. Cacophony
6. Cadence
7. Cajole
8. Callous
9. Calumny
10. Camaraderie

LESSON EIGHT

A. Dictation

_____ /10

B. Fill in the blanks with the most appropriate words

01 The camp fosters a sense of both independence and _____ among its members.

02 He gave me a _____ "goodbye", and I wondered if I had done something to annoy him.

03 The storm triggered a _____ of car alarms that blared like a warning through the streets.

04 The swordsman _____ the attack with his own parry.

05 A witch is often thought to be a _____ old woman who enjoys hurting people.

06 The prosecutor's blatant _____ toward the victim was reported by every news organization.

07 We had a _____ at our wedding because it was cheaper than doing a three-course meal.

08 He tried to _____ me into going on the roller coaster, but I refused.

09 The town _____ into a thriving, colourful city.

10 The guitarist played a blues riff to the _____ set by the drummer.

LESSON NINE

Target Words

1. Canvas
2. Capricious
3. Captivate
4. Carouse
5. Cavity
6. Cavort
7. Celestial
8. Chastise
9. Choreographed
10. Circumlocution

LESSON NINE

A. Dictation

____/10

B. Fill in the blanks with the most appropriate words

01 The dentist told me that despite all my flossing, I still had three _____ in my teeth.

02 The girls _____ across the wheat field, enjoying the warm of the sun.

03 All the critics thought the movie was _____ and lauded it for being so engaging.

04 A celebration was in order, so they bought champagne and _____ all evening.

05 The ballet dancer practiced the _____ sequence to perfection.

06 Andrew used acrylic and oil paint on _____ as his main medium.

07 The killer's confession came after years of _____ and dishonesty.

08 We were _____ for not wearing our school uniforms.

09 The _____ map depicts the location of various astronomical sights in the night sky.

10 His _____ nature makes him prone to flights of fancy.

LESSON TEN

Target Words

1. Circumspect
2. Clairvoyant
3. Claustrophobia
4. Cliché
5. Coalesce
6. Cogent
7. Collusion
8. Colossus
9. Comatose
10. Commendable

LESSON TEN

A. Dictation

____ /10

B. Fill in the blanks with the most appropriate words

01 The company was accused of _____ and was investigated by the FBI for conspiracy.

02 Esmeralda is a _____ and claims she can see the future.

03 I don't like going in elevators because I have severe _____.

04 If we give our inspiration a moment to _____, we can create something much greater together.

05 Jack was _____ after a sixteen-hour work shift. He slept until evening the next day!

06 "Smart as a whip" and "ignorance is bliss" are tired _____ we should put to rest.

07 The police officer was very _____ when wording his public confession.

08 My _____ professor has been a biology researcher for twenty-six years.

09 The _____ towered before us, casting an enormous shadow over everything.

10 His brave and _____ actions in the war won him a medal of honour.

LESSON ELEVEN

Target Words

1. Commodious
2. Compel
3. Complicit
4. Compliment
5. Concede
6. Conciliatory
7. Concoct
8. Concord
9. Conduit
10. Confluence

LESSON ELEVEN

A. Dictation

____ /10

B. Fill in the blanks with the most appropriate words

01 After much disagreement, I finally _____ and admitted he was right.

02 The witch _____ an evil plan to make the princess fall asleep forever.

03 Under the English Channel is a _____ that connects the UK and France.

04 Jason had a _____ meeting with his superiors, who happily promoted him.

05 I cannot _____ him to be smarter, but I can ask him to study more often.

06 Her _____ about my outfit made me happy for the rest of the night.

07 A _____ between the two warring countries brought peace and prosperity to both.

08 Casey was _____ in the robbery, so she was sentenced to five years in prison.

09 My mom's new minivan is quite _____. All five of my siblings can fit in it comfortably!

10 We reached a _____ about who would take out the trash on Sundays.

LESSON TWELVE

Target Words

1. Confound
2. Connotation
3. Contusion
4. Convalescence
5. Copious
6. Corpulent
7. Cosmopolitan
8. Credulity
9. Cursory
10. Daft

LESSON TWELVE

A. Dictation

_____ /10

B. Fill in the blanks with the most appropriate words

01 Her _____ and very public remark about the earth being flat gave me second-hand embarrassment.

02 A _____ made by the interviewer suggested the athlete was using performance-enhancing drugs.

03 Celeste is a _____ woman who is well traveled, well read, and well spoken.

04 I fell down the stairs and was left with a painful, purple _____ on my knee.

05 Some say _____ is a sign of being gullible, but Marla thinks it's a sign of optimism.

06 To everyone's surprise, the once-sinewy fitness instructor had become quite a _____ man.

07 The policeman gave me a _____ glance as he looked through my files, which made me feel nervous.

08 The buffet at our wedding will have _____ amounts of vegetarian options.

09 I was so happy to hear of Tim's _____ after he was diagnosed with cancer.

10 The riddle _____ most people, but a few clever folks will figure it out.

LESSON THIRTEEN

Target Words

1. Daunting
2. Dearth
3. Defame
4. Deft
5. Defunct
6. Deleterious
7. Delude
8. Deluge
9. Derelict
10. Desolate

LESSON THIRTEEN

A. Dictation

____/10

B. Fill in the blanks with the most appropriate words

01 Elizabeth's comments about my appearance were _____ and left me in tears.

02 Deserts are considered _____ places, but in reality they are teeming with life!

03 He had a _____ hand when it came to playing any type of card game.

04 Conspiracy theories often _____ or completely obscure the truth.

05 The realization that she would never love me hit me like a _____.

06 Though the tabloids try to _____ celebrities, some are able to rise above and ignore the lies.

07 Our country has a _____ of multilingual people. No one here can speak more than one language!

08 The school had become _____ over the years: windows were shattered, and doors were boarded up.

09 Taking the SATs can be _____, but you'll feel better if you study hard!

10 Landline telephones have become mostly _____, and for some they are totally obsolete.

LESSON FOURTEEN

Target Words

1. Despondent
2. Destitute
3. Diaphanous
4. Dictate
5. Differentiate
6. Dilapidated
7. Diligent
8. Diminish
9. Diminutive
10. Discreet

LESSON FOURTEEN

A. Dictation

____/10

B. Fill in the blanks with the most appropriate words

01 The cobwebs were _____, sparkling in the sunshine and wavering gently in the breeze.

02 There is a _____ house on Neibolt Street that everyone thinks is haunted.

03 The Meyers Twins are hard to _____ because they are identical!

04 He tried to blow his nose _____ but garnered irritated looks from other people in the class.

05 After his dog died, Brian was _____ and soon fell into a state of deep depression.

06 That part of town is _____, being inhabited primarily by the homeless.

07 The congressman _____ a strange new policy that would prohibit the sale of spray paint.

08 Amanda is _____ when it comes to school projects and almost always gets an A.

09 She showed me a _____ model of her old house that she had been working on for months.

10 He _____ my accomplishment by claiming that writing a book wasn't that hard.

LESSON FIFTEEN

Target Words

1. Discrete
2. Disparage
3. Dissonance
4. Divergent
5. Diverse
6. Divisive
7. Domicile
8. Doppelgänger
9. Douse
10. Dutiful

LESSON FIFTEEN

A. Dictation

____ /10

B. Fill in the blanks with the most appropriate words

01 She _____ herself in perfume before leaving for the party.

02 The company is made up of four _____ departments.

03 The film is _____ among critics. Some people find it offensive, while others find it intriguing.

04 Cara doesn't like people visiting her _____ because she considers it her private space.

05 The new hire was a _____ of my old college roommate. They could have been twins!

06 The coach _____ the team, telling them the loss was no one's fault but their own.

07 The New Yorker magazine covers a _____ range of topics.

08 I went to a symphony but didn't enjoy it because the amateur orchestra was plagued by _____ and a complete lack of rhythm.

09 The test subject was _____ in that he had a completely unique reaction to the therapy session.

10 Ryan is a _____ employee who fulfills his responsibilities no matter what.

LESSON SIXTEEN

Target Words

1. Dynamic
2. Elocution
3. Elucidate
4. Empathetic
5. Empathy
6. Enervate
7. Enervated
8. Entity
9. Entomology
10. Envious

LESSON SIXTEEN

A. Dictation

____ /10

B. Fill in the blanks with the most appropriate words

01 I have a lot of _____ for people who have anxiety because it used to plague me as well!

02 She is an _____ young woman who has a lot of compassion for others.

03 I was _____ after running the half-marathon.

04 Joe was the handsomest guy in their group of friends, and Mark often felt _____ of him.

05 Politicians must master the art of _____ because addressing the public is part of the job!

06 Walking up two dozen flights of stairs will _____ even the most physically fit people.

07 Her writing style is _____ and ever-evolving. It changes slightly with every book she publishes.

08 The reporter asked the mayor to _____ his ridiculous claim that all teenagers are troublemakers.

09 Dr. Bug studies _____, which is quite fitting, considering his name!

10 The rabbi does not think of God as a physical _____. Rather, he views God as an omnipotent being.

LESSON SEVENTEEN

Target Words

1. Erect
2. Erroneous
3. Espouse
4. Espy
5. Ethereal
6. Euphoric
7. Exacerbate
8. Excursion
9. Exemplary
10. Exigent

LESSON SEVENTEEN

A. Dictation

____ /10

B. Fill in the blanks with the most appropriate words

01 The gala was held in an _____ mansion with roses decorating the spiral staircase in the foyer.

02 The fight was _____ when a tornado trapped them both in the underpass.

03 She is an _____ member of the military. All the commanders think she is exceptional.

04 His _____ assumptions ended up making him look silly.

05 We book _____ when we go on cruises, so that we can go on adventures while the ship is docked.

06 I could _____ flakes of snow falling through the crack in my window.

07 They _____ a monument in his honor in the town square.

08 We _____ his claim that he was innocent, because we knew he was telling the truth.

09 I felt _____ on my wedding day. It was the happiest day of my life.

10 There was an _____ announcement on the TV, forecasting a violent storm.

LESSON EIGHTEEN

Target Words

1. Existential
2. Exorbitant
3. Extol
4. Extravagant
5. Fabricate
6. Fabulist
7. Facile
8. Fallacious
9. Familial
10. Fatuous

LESSON EIGHTEEN

A. Dictation

____/10

B. Fill in the blanks with the most appropriate words

01 The mother scolded her young children for acting so _____ during the church service.

02 I wouldn't necessarily call him a _____, but he definitely embellishes details.

03 Our charity organization was _____ for helping clean up the city and raise awareness to prevent littering and pollution.

04 The writer is an expert at _____ new, exciting stories. She has sold millions of books.

05 My TV wasn't working, but it was a _____ issue that only took a few minutes to fix.

06 We drank _____ amounts of orange juice that morning and felt quite sick afterwards.

07 The _____ news headline led many people to feel worried and confused.

08 Some people think _____ relationships are more important than friends or coworkers.

09 The art installation depicts _____ dread, and fear of being alone in the universe.

10 Our Halloween party will be an _____ event with lots of games, music, and a huge buffet!

LESSON NINETEEN

Target Words

1. Fecund
2. Feign
3. Feral
4. Fetter
5. Fey
6. Fickle
7. Figurative
8. Firmament
9. Flabbergasted
10. Flaccid

LESSON NINETEEN

A. Dictation

_____/10

B. Fill in the blanks with the most appropriate words

01. My friend Azumi can be _____. She often cancels plans without much notice.

02. I extended a _____ olive branch, but he threw it right back at me!

03. After a rainy summer, the soil was _____ and ready to grow a bountiful harvest.

04. We found a _____ clearing in the woods that looked as if it had once been home to forest nymphs.

05. He _____ interest throughout the interview and was glad when it ended.

06. I lay on the hill and gazed up at the _____ twinkling in the dusk.

07. The plant had gone _____ and wilted after being deprived of water for weeks.

08. She was _____ to learn that her best friend had stolen her history essay.

09. Some cats are _____ and do not like humans.

10. The prisoner sat in the back of the dungeon, _____ with iron shackles.

LESSON TWENTY

Target Words

1. Flattery
2. Flout
3. Fluctuate
4. Flux
5. Forage
6. Forestall
7. Forlorn
8. Formidable
9. Forsake
10. Fortify

LESSON TWENTY

A. Dictation

____ /10

B. Fill in the blanks with the most appropriate words

01 The administration is in a state of _____ because a new board of directors is being appointed.

02 After the shipwreck, Russ was marooned on a deserted island. He felt as if God had _____ him.

03 Squirrels _____ for nuts and store them in hiding places for the winter months.

04 You cannot _____ the exam just because you didn't study! Ready or not, you have to take it.

05 The river current _____ with the seasons. It flows much slower in winter than it does in spring.

06 We _____ our cause by recruiting new members and spreading awareness.

07 Sasha tried _____ on the police officer that pulled her over, but to no avail.

08 Michael admitted to knowingly and willingly _____ laws against armed robbery.

09 My team is competing against the _____ champions of last year's competition.

10 After his girlfriend broke up with him, Jacob was so _____ he didn't leave his house for five days.

LESSON TWENTY-ONE

Target Words

1. Fortitude
2. Fortuitous
3. Foster
4. Frenetic
5. Gape
6. Gay
7. Gluttonous
8. Goad
9. Gourmand
10. Grandiose

LESSON TWENTY-ONE

A. Dictation

____ /10

B. Fill in the blanks with the most appropriate words

01 It was a _____ job offer that he knew was once-in-a-lifetime opportunity.

02 Her four-year-old son did a backflip, and all she could do was _____ at him in shock.

03 Uncle Reed is a _____. He has travelled all over the world just to try exotic foods.

04 Kelly tried to be strong, but in the face of defeat, her _____ was wavering.

05 The vice president _____ the president into offering their employees a Christmas bonus.

06 Christmas was coming. The streets were _____ and full of people.

07 The school hopes to _____ a sense of community among its students.

08 Her _____ energy made me anxious, so I asked her to calm down.

09 Being _____ can have major consequences. Overeating often causes diabetes and weight gain.

10 They live in a _____ mansion secluded up on a hill. They have two pools and a tennis court!

LESSON TWENTY-TWO

Target Words

1. Gregarious
2. Grotto
3. Guile
4. Hail
5. Hapless
6. Harmony
7. Harrowing
8. Hedonist
9. Henchman
10. Hiatus

LESSON TWENTY-TWO

A. Dictation

____ /10

B. Fill in the blanks with the most appropriate words

01 The runner had to take a _____ from competing after he sprained his ankle.

02 Henry used his natural cunning and _____ to get out of tricky situations.

03 My new roommate is quite _____. She goes to so many parties!

04 Bekah _____ from a rural part of town a few hours outside of Atlanta.

05 The evil scientist ordered his _____ to bring him an unsuspecting victim.

06 My cousin has had a _____ year; he lost his job, divorced his wife, and broke his arm.

07 The girls' voices were in perfect _____. One was a soprano, and the other was an alto.

08 Rats scurried into the _____ to take shelter from the storm.

09 My self-indulgent sister lives the life of a _____.

10 The award-winning documentary was a _____ piece about racism in America.

LESSON TWENTY-THREE

Target Words

1. Hibernal
2. Hierarchy
3. Histrionic
4. Idolatrous
5. Illusory
6. Immaculate
7. Immutable
8. Impecunious
9. Impervious
10. Impudent

LESSON TWENTY-THREE

A. Dictation

____ /10

B. Fill in the blanks with the most appropriate words

01 There is a clear _____ in the company, and staff writers are at the lowest tier.

02 I made sure my apartment was _____ before my friends came over.

03 The student's _____ behaviour earned her detention.

04 The frigid, _____ weather made Eloise want to stay inside her warm house all day.

05 Fashion is not _____. It is always changing to fit current trends.

06 My cousin can be _____ when she gets into a heated argument with someone.

07 Mike is _____ to their insults. He has developed thick skin.

08 Nellie's parents were worried about her _____ relationship with her new boyfriend. She treated him like a saint instead of a regular guy.

09 The _____ neighbourhood on the outskirts of town is susceptible to high rates of crime.

10 Mr. Mage the magician put on a show that displayed his most incredible tricks. Most of his magic was, of course, _____.

LESSON TWENTY-FOUR

Target Words

1. Incessant
2. Incisive
3. Inclement
4. Inclination
5. Indictment
6. Indignation
7. Inextricable
8. Infuse
9. Ingenious
10. Inimical

LESSON TWENTY-FOUR

A. Dictation

____ /10

B. Fill in the blanks with the most appropriate words

01 His _____ remark left me worried for my life!

02 My neighbor has a dog whose _____ barking wakes me up almost every morning.

03 An _____ was made against the CEO. He had stolen thousands of dollars from his own company!

04 We planned an outdoor party but the _____ weather may force us to reschedule.

05 This honey is _____ with lavender, and it's perfect to put in Earl Grey tea.

06 The turtle was caught in a fishing net, seemingly _____, but the rescuers were eventually able to cut him loose.

07 Thanks to the _____ contributions of past inventors, technology has come a long way.

08 The _____ professor can catch a student cheating from fifty feet away.

09 He is a scientist by _____ and a researcher by choice.

10 She couldn't suppress a feeling of _____ after being disqualified for ludicrous reasons.

LESSON TWENTY-FIVE

Target Words

1. Iniquity
2. Innate
3. Innocuous
4. Inquisitor
5. Inundate
6. Invariable
7. Invective
8. Inveterate
9. Irascible
10. Jubilant

LESSON TWENTY-FIVE

A. Dictation

____/10

B. Fill in the blanks with the most appropriate words

01 Tyler's _____ mother always seems annoyed when he has friends over.

02 The town was _____ after the dam burst.

03 Though raccoons may look _____, they are wild animals and should not be bothered!

04 The prosecutor launched _____ at the witness, who broke down in tears and admitted that she had lied on the stand.

05 The wedding was a _____ event that we will treasure for the rest of our lives.

06 For the experiment, the researchers created a control group that would remain _____.

07 Her soccer skills are seemingly _____. She has always been an excellent player!

08 The reveal of the ambassador's past _____ was big news. No one expected he was a murderer!

09 Uncle Ricky is an _____ gambler. He has struggled with his addiction for years.

10 The _____ went door to door asking civilians if they had seen the kidnapper.

LESSON TWENTY-SIX

Target Words

1. Judicious
2. Juvenile
3. Juxtapose
4. Labyrinthine
5. Laceration
6. Lachrymose
7. Latent
8. Laud
9. Laudatory
10. Lavish

LESSON TWENTY-SIX

A. Dictation

____/10

B. Fill in the blanks with the most appropriate words

01 The poem _____ the vivacity of the forest with the desolation of the desert.

02 She became bored with the _____ conversation and left to talk to someone more mature.

03 The _____ university is easy to get lost in. It's a huge campus!

04 They threw a _____ baby shower for their sister, complete with an entire wall of fresh roses.

05 His _____ and cool-headed evaluation of the crisis helped him save many lives that day.

06 Much to Ben's horror, his _____ plea for a prom date was broadcast all over social media.

07 My teacher's _____ comments, written at the end of my paper, made me very happy.

08 After stomping through thorny bushes, Kelly had multiple _____ on her legs.

09 Our parents _____ our good grades. They give us monthly allowance as a reward!

10 She has a _____ disregard for authority that will become a problem later in life.

LESSON TWENTY-SEVEN

Target Words

1. Lethargic
2. Lewd
3. Libel
4. Licentious
5. Limber
6. Limpid
7. Linchpin
8. Lithe
9. Loquacious
10. Lull

LESSON TWENTY-SEVEN

A. Dictation

____ /10

B. Fill in the blanks with the most appropriate words

01 The marathon runner felt very _____ after running so much the day before.

02 Be careful of Jerry. He is a _____ man with few morals.

03 A driver cut Tim off during rush hour and proceeded to flash a _____ hand gesture at him.

04 The coffee shop experiences a _____ around noon, which is when many people are out to lunch.

05 James is the _____ of the company. Without him, the whole thing would collapse.

06 The dancer's _____ frame allows her to move and bend as fluidly as water.

07 The president accused the journalist of _____ and demanded the online article be taken down.

08 Yew is a very pliable, _____ wood that is easy to work with.

09 The lake was _____. You could see all the way to the bottom!

10 Debby is my _____ new roommate. She's going to talk my ears off!

LESSON TWENTY-EIGHT

Target Words

1. Luminescence
2. Magnanimous
3. Malaise
4. Malevolent
5. Malicious
6. Malign
7. Malleable
8. Mandatory
9. Manifest
10. Manifold

LESSON TWENTY-EIGHT

A. Dictation

____/10

B. Fill in the blanks with the most appropriate words

01 Dr. Stein made _____ financial contributions to the university.

02 We have a _____ work meeting today. You cannot miss it!

03 She had _____ reasons for being frightened of bugs.

04 I warned him not to _____ my best friend in my presence.

05 He _____ obvious signs of anxiety and depression.

06 Working at the shoe factory every day for twelve hours was a tiresome _____.

07 The artist uses _____ metals and wood to make his art.

08 There was a _____ quality to his smirk that sent chills down my spine.

09 The prank was _____. There was nothing lighthearted about it.

10 There is a _____ to her skin that is otherworldly.

LESSON TWENTY-NINE

Target Words

1. Masticate
2. Matrimony
3. Maudlin
4. Maxim
5. Meagre (US Meager)
6. Mediate
7. Melodramatic
8. Mendacious
9. Mercurial
10. Meritorious

LESSON TWENTY-NINE

A. Dictation

____ /10

B. Fill in the blanks with the most appropriate words

01. The wine made her _____, and she professed her love to all her friends.

02. Billy's science project won first place due to his _____ efforts and creativity.

03. The referee attempted to _____ the argument between the two soccer players.

04. I try to stay away from _____ people. Dishonesty is a plague in any relationship.

05. If you don't _____ your food properly before swallowing, you might choke!

06. She looked from her sister's huge plate of food to her own _____ serving and wondered why she had been snubbed.

07. The couple was joined in _____ in a beautiful church.

08. He muttered his favourite _____ under his breath for strength, and then stepped out on the stage.

09. Though I only stepped on her foot, her cry was so _____ that you'd think I'd broken every toe!

10. Her _____ disposition made it difficult for her to find work. One minute she was cheerful and polite, but the next she was glum and impudent.

LESSON THIRTY

Target Words

1. Metamorphosis
2. Mimic
3. Misogyny
4. Modicum
5. Mollify
6. Monogamy
7. Mores
8. Morose
9. Munificent
10. Mutability

LESSON THIRTY

A. Dictation

____ /10

B. Fill in the blanks with the most appropriate words

01 Doing yoga every day has helped _____ Claire's temperamental disposition.

02 He does not have even a _____ of respect for his superiors.

03 I was jubilant to hear of his _____ donation to our cause.

04 Her _____ concerning shark hunting changed after she saw the documentary.

05 He was fired for blatant display of _____ against the women in the office.

06 The caterpillar's incredible _____ into a butterfly is nature at its finest.

07 The cold, incessantly rainy weather of February always makes me a bit _____.

08 Paul doesn't believe in _____, so he'll probably never get married!

09 Her _____ allows her to work a job that requires annual relocations.

10 Cara _____ the effortless French fashion of Brigitte Bardot.

LESSON THIRTY-ONE

Target Words

1. Myopic
2. Myriad
3. Narrate
4. Nebulous
5. Nefarious
6. Neologism
7. Neonate
8. Noisome
9. Notoriety
10. Novel

LESSON THIRTY-ONE

A. Dictation

____/10

B. Fill in the blanks with the most appropriate words

01 The _____ vapours from the toxic waste led many people to move away.

02 Clarice went to the eye doctor because she was _____. She couldn't see very far.

03 The _____ ideas he had about bolstering the economy won him many supporters.

04 The warlock gave the princess a wedding gift, but his intentions were _____.

05 David Attenborough _____ the BBC series Planet Earth.

06 The celebrity attracted some _____ after divorcing her husband of only twenty-two days.

07 The writer showed me his library, which contained _____ books in many different genres.

08 My sister gave birth last week. Her little _____ was born with a full head of hair!

09 Paris Hilton could be considered an entrepreneur of _____ after she coined the iconic valley girl phrase, "That's hot."

10 The artist tries to convey his opinions of love and life, but it comes across as somewhat _____.

LESSON THIRTY-TWO

Target Words

1. Noxious
2. Obdurate
3. Obfuscate
4. Obsequious
5. Odious
6. Officious
7. Olfactory
8. Ominous
9. Oration
10. Ostracize

LESSON THIRTY-TWO

A. Dictation

____ /10

B. Fill in the blanks with the most appropriate words

01 My _____ sister always wants to be of help, but sometimes she just gets in the way.

02 If you weren't so stubborn and _____, you'd see that I'm trying to help!

03 The _____ storm clouds grew closer. People shuttered their windows and took shelter.

04 For centuries, Jews have been ridiculed, _____, and even hunted. Anti-Semitism is a disease that must be cured!

05 The student's paper is riddled with spelling and grammar errors that _____ his essay entirely.

06 It is in Meg's nature to be _____. She obeys every rule and is rarely truculent.

07 The _____ fumes coming out of the pipes can cause many health problems.

08 The new king is an _____ young man who is as cruel as he is ugly.

09 A dog's _____ senses far surpass those of a human's.

10 He was gifted in the art of _____ and could captivate a room full of people with the way he told stories.

LESSON THIRTY-THREE

Target Words

1. Pacify
2. Paragon
3. Pariah
4. Parody
5. Patent
6. Pedagogue
7. Pellucid
8. Penchant
9. Peregrinate
10. Perfunctory

LESSON THIRTY-THREE

A. Dictation

____/10

B. Fill in the blanks with the most appropriate words

01. Sara had longed to be a _____ since she was eleven years old, and today she would graduate from the university's teaching program!

02. Some people treat him like a _____, but he's neither rebel nor outsider.

03. I tried to _____ her anger and frustration with a cup of chamomile tea.

04. Leah was sick of being a housekeeper, but she completed her shift with _____ compliance, nonetheless.

05. Ernest Hemingway is known for his straightforward, _____ style of writing.

06. My mom has a _____ for knowing when rain is on the way: she always gets a blinding headache!

07. *Saturday Night Live* is known for its satirical comedy and making _____ of current events.

08. Jack Kerouac's *On the Road* follows a group of free spirits who _____ across the US.

09. The American Olympian Simone Biles is a _____ of athleticism and self-discipline.

10. Her _____ attempt to cheat on the final exam earned her a failing grade.

LESSON THIRTY-FOUR

Target Words

1. Permeate
2. Persevere
3. Pertinacious
4. Peruse
5. Pervasive
6. Petulance
7. Physiognomy
8. Pique
9. Pithy
10. Pittance

LESSON THIRTY-FOUR

A. Dictation

____ /10

B. Fill in the blanks with the most appropriate words

01 Prejudice is unfortunately quite _____ in most societies.

02 She gave a short, poignant, and _____ presentation about the perils of hiking alone.

03 He broke up with her, so she left the restaurant in a _____ state.

04 My _____ cousin insisted on taking the long route, despite our protests.

05 You do not have a _____ of respect for your elders!

06 The runner paced himself. He knew he had to _____ to the end of the marathon.

07 The bonfire next door _____ the air and wafted into my apartment.

08 Eloise _____ the selection of old National Geographic magazines.

09 _____ isn't a strictly scientific practice. Many scientists rebuke it.

10 His daughter's constant _____ was cause for much stress and fatigue.

LESSON THIRTY-FIVE

Target Words

1. Placate
2. Placid
3. Plethora
4. Pliable
5. Poach
6. Poised
7. Polygamy
8. Portentous
9. Portly
10. Precarious

LESSON THIRTY-FIVE

A. Dictation

____ /10

B. Fill in the blanks with the most appropriate words

01. The lake below looked _____ from their quiet spot on top of the mountain.

02. The ballerina stood _____, ready to step out on stage for her performance.

03. I love my university because it has a _____ of classes to choose from!

04. The man was put in prison for _____ an endangered species of whale.

05. I picked up the envelope, unaware that its _____ contents would change my life for the worse.

06. Rosa, Adrian, and Doug practice _____. They are all in a romantic relationship with one another!

07. After having coffee spilled on her, my sister was livid, so I tried to _____ her rage.

08. The jeweller uses _____ metals to make stunning pairs of earrings.

09. The tabloids slammed the young movie star for his new, _____ appearance.

10. I climbed up the _____ ladder, praying to God it wouldn't tip over.

LESSON THIRTY-SIX

Target Words

1. Predestination
2. Premonition
3. Preponderance
4. Presage
5. Prestidigitation
6. Presumptuous
7. Profane
8. Profuse
9. Propensity
10. Propriety

LESSON THIRTY-SIX

A. Dictation

____/10

B. Fill in the blanks with the most appropriate words

01 The _____ language used in the film earned it an R rating.

02 The blisters were an unfortunate _____ of his illness returning.

03 Mike the Magician is skilled in the art of _____ and illusion.

04 Lola doesn't believe in _____. She believes a person can make his or her own destiny.

05 Barry's _____ behaviour towards the women in his workplace will get him fired one day.

06 I want to know why there is a _____ of women in post-secondary education.

07 The Victorian Era was dominated by _____ and strong moral sensibilities.

08 Victoria has a _____ for numbers, so it's no wonder she is an accountant!

09 The fortune-teller had a _____ about Robin's future. She claimed Robin would be married within the next year!

10 The Kardashian family is known for their _____ wealth and scripted reality drama.

LESSON THIRTY-SEVEN

Target Words

1. Protean
2. Prudent
3. Puerile
4. Pugnacious
5. Pulchritude
6. Punctilious
7. Pungent
8. Purport
9. Putrid
10. Quaint

LESSON THIRTY-SEVEN

A. Dictation

____/10

B. Fill in the blanks with the most appropriate words

01 Some cheeses have a _____ smell that you'll find either enticing or off-putting.

02 The painter was in awe of her _____ and begged her to let him paint her portrait.

03 There is a _____ smell coming from the garbage that reeks like rotten eggs.

04 The teacher reprimanded the trouble-making group of boys for their _____ class behaviour.

05 Tracy is a _____ young woman who never steps out of line.

06 Elias and Erin stayed in a _____ bed and breakfast on their trip to Marseille.

07 She is a _____ filmmaker whose films encompass a wide range of styles and genre.

08 You should be more _____ when climbing these steep stairs. You could fall down!

09 He _____ to be innocent, but everyone knows it's a lie.

10 The security guard kicked out two drunken men for being _____.

LESSON THIRTY-EIGHT

Target Words

1. Quid pro quo
2. Quotidian
3. Radiant
4. Rancid
5. Ratiocinate
6. Raze
7. Recalcitrant
8. Recalibrate
9. Recapitulate
10. Rectify

LESSON THIRTY-EIGHT

A. Dictation

____/10

B. Fill in the blanks with the most appropriate words

01 Don loves his _____ newspaper delivery service. He reads the paper every day!

02 She looked _____ in the sequin dress. Light danced off her like a rainbow.

03 A fallen missile _____ the farmer's crops. He was devastated.

04 Your _____ behaviour could get you in trouble. Try being more cooperative!

05 The lawyer _____ his statement because the judge didn't hear him.

06 She accidentally left her wet clothes in the washing machine for three days. They were _____.

07 The GPS system had to _____ after we took a wrong turn.

08 The doctor proposed a _____ to the FBI agent. They could help one another.

09 The jurors were left in a room to _____ over the evidence and appeals they had heard.

10 He hoped to _____ his past wrongdoings by facing his demons head-on.

LESSON THIRTY-NINE

Target Words

1. Redact
2. Redoubtable
3. Redress
4. Reel
5. Refrain
6. Reiterate
7. Relish
8. Remiss
9. Render
10. Renovate

LESSON THIRTY-NINE

A. Dictation

_____ /10

B. Fill in the blanks with the most appropriate words

01 Riding the merry-go-round makes my head _____.

02 The governor promised to _____ the increasing unemployment rate.

03 The anaesthesia _____ him unconscious in a matter of seconds.

04 I had to _____ from punching him after he called my friend ugly.

05 Tara loves the beach. She _____ the feeling of warm sand on her skin.

06 The _____ soldier was promoted to the rank of officer and given a special medal.

07 She asked him to _____ his point because he had gone a bit off topic.

08 You would be _____ not to attend the job fair this Saturday.

09 The old mansion on the hill is being _____ to restore its original beauty.

10 The scholar tried to _____ his racist sentiments, but they had been broadcast live!

LESSON FORTY

Target Words

1. Repose
2. Reprehensible
3. Repudiate
4. Repulse
5. Requisition
6. Restitution
7. Retaliation
8. Retract
9. Retribution
10. Revel (in)

LESSON FORTY

A. Dictation

____/10

B. Fill in the blanks with the most appropriate words

01 The director did a _____ job on his documentary, and deserves to be panned by critics!

02 Melanie _____ Mark's flirtatious advances because she already had a boyfriend.

03 The swordsman _____ his blade from the scabbard and stood en garde.

04 If you don't pay your taxes, the IRS will _____ your belongings.

05 Kelly was seeking _____ for yesterday's public embarrassment, which had been concocted by the malevolent Mary Jo.

06 My sister is _____ by creatures with many too many legs, such as spiders and centipedes.

07 Mr. Jenkins just wants some peaceful _____, but his neighbours are partying like the world is ending!

08 He has invited _____ by messing with the wrong people.

09 Rob isn't very kind. He _____ in seeing his friends humiliated.

10 Ellen was ordered to pay $200 in _____ for drawing graffiti on a public building.

LESSON FORTY-ONE

Target Words

1. Rife
2. Ruddy
3. Ruse
4. Rustic
5. Saccharine
6. Sacrosanct
7. Sagacious
8. Salient
9. Salutation
10. Sanguine

LESSON FORTY-ONE

A. Dictation

____ /10

B. Fill in the blanks with the most appropriate words

01 The farmhouse was decorated in a _____ style to reflect the pastoral scenery.

02 The Old Testament is a _____ part of the Bible used in both Christianity and Judaism.

03 Her presentation on global warming covered every _____ subtopic of the crisis.

04 Shaking hands is a common _____ in many parts of the world.

05 Ellie tried to come up with a clever _____ to make her roommate do the dishes.

06 She has a _____ auburn hair colour that shines bright red in the sunlight.

07 The library is _____ with geography books.

08 My aunt makes the most _____ brownies you'll ever taste. They're so rich in flavour that it's difficult to eat more than one!

09 Todd made many thoughtful, _____ decisions when he decided to move across the country.

10 Watching It's a Wonderful Life put me in a very _____ Christmas mood!

LESSON FORTY-TWO

Target Words

1. Sate
2. Satiate
3. Savour
4. Scathing
5. Scourge
6. Scurrilous
7. Sedate
8. Sedentary
9. Seer
10. Seminal

LESSON FORTY-TWO

A. Dictation

_____/10

B. Fill in the blanks with the most appropriate words

01 The staff at the zoo had to _____ the tiger after it tried to attack its trainer.

02 I read a _____ review of the new Star Wars film, so I decided not to see it.

03 After I devoured two cheeseburgers and a milkshake, my hunger was _____.

04 A _____ research paper about Alzheimer's disease led to exciting new breakthroughs.

05 Serena _____ the wine. It was expensive and delicious.

06 He is in poor health because he has a very lazy, _____ lifestyle.

07 His _____ comments about my weight gain made me cry!

08 The _____ told us to be careful driving next week because she had a premonition of a car accident!

09 Locusts are a _____ on crops. They can destroy entire harvests!

10 The man _____ his desire for a fancy car by purchasing a Lamborghini on a whim!

LESSON FORTY-THREE

Target Words

1. Serendipity
2. Slander
3. Sobriety
4. Somnolent
5. Sordid
6. Soothsayer
7. Spectral
8. Spurious
9. Stagnant
10. Stagnate

LESSON FORTY-THREE

A. Dictation

___/10

B. Fill in the blanks with the most appropriate words

01. The celebrity is suing the tabloid for _____. She claims their article has hurt her career.

02. We are going to speak with the _____ to see if she can tell us our future.

03. His election campaign _____ after his campaign manager made some careless public remarks.

04. It was _____ that kept her from getting on the airplane that later crashed.

05. Even though I have drunk four cups of coffee today, I still feel _____.

06. The "mockumentary," a _____ subgenre of documentaries, has gained popularity in recent years.

07. After years as an alcoholic, Charles took up _____ in hopes it might turn his life around.

08. I saw a pale, _____ form in the window of the supposedly haunted mansion.

09. The ox stood _____ in the middle of the road, totally unaware of the traffic jam it had caused.

10. His _____ attempt at winning her affection was creepy at best.

LESSON FORTY-FOUR

Target Words

1. Static
2. Steadfast
3. Strenuous
4. Strife
5. Stupefy
6. Submissive
7. Subsist
8. Succinct
9. Suffice
10. Supplant

LESSON FORTY-FOUR

A. Dictation

____/10

B. Fill in the blanks with the most appropriate words

01 He was _____ in his decision to remain on the island alone.

02 There was an excited, _____ buzz in the room that sounded like the steady hum of bees.

03 You cannot _____ on a diet of only pizza and soda. Eventually, you would experience the effects of malnutrition.

04 The magician _____ his audience by narrowly escaping the perilous underwater cage.

05 The continuous _____ over the last year has left me haggard and hopeless.

06 After the host's lengthy introductory monologue, the other presenters' speeches seemed _____ by comparison.

07 The prisoner knew how terrible solitary confinement could be, so he acted very _____ towards the guards in order to avoid experiencing such horrendous, prolonged solitude.

08 Writing a thesis or dissertation is a _____ and demanding aspect of most graduate programs.

09 The assignment was to write a 10,000-word essay, so his meagre two-page report will not _____.

10 By studying harder than ever before, Bradley intended to _____ his brother as the smartest boy in the family.

LESSON FORTY-FIVE

Target Words

1. Surfeit
2. Surmise
3. Surreptitious
4. Swarthy
5. Sybarite
6. Sycophant
7. Sympathetic
8. Sympathy
9. Synopsis
10. Taciturn

LESSON FORTY-FIVE

A. Dictation

____ /10

B. Fill in the blanks with the most appropriate words

01 My _____ grandparents live in an elegant mansion in the Italian countryside.

02 She _____ the best solution for her problem by carefully considering every option.

03 Uncle James made a _____ of pasta for our family dinner. We were all stuffed!

04 Some think librarians are strict and _____ by default, but they are normal people too!

05 I felt _____ about his inability to afford a car, so I let him borrow mine.

06 The student looked for a _____ for the English book he had neglected to read.

07 He is coldhearted and has no _____ for those in need.

08 Elia's dark hair, brown eyes, and _____ olive complexion made her a classic Italian beauty.

09 This man is nothing but a _____! Don't pay attention to his underhanded cajolery!

10 The illicit organization holds their _____ meetings in the most inconspicuous places.

LESSON FORTY-SIX

Target Words

1. Tantamount
2. Tedious
3. Telepathic
4. Tenuous
5. Terrestrial
6. Terse
7. Timorous
8. Tome
9. Toothsome
10. Torpid

LESSON FORTY-SIX

A. Dictation

____/10

B. Fill in the blanks with the most appropriate words

01 The _____ hippopotamus took heavy, languid steps out of the pool.

02 The print-only newspaper has a _____ hold on its readership in the age of blogs and social media.

03 The CDC official offered a _____ and somewhat vague explanation for the sudden viral outbreak, which did little to calm the public's nerves.

04 My calculus professor's monotonous voice made for a very _____ class.

05 She has a nearly _____ ability to detect people's deepest insecurities.

06 In the eyes of many voters, the candidate's careless remarks about the military were _____ to treason.

07 Evolution caused some aquatic animals to become _____ over thousands of years.

08 The dog in the shelter gave me one _____ look, and I knew I had to take him in.

09 The entrée at the wedding was especially _____. I wish I could have gotten the recipe!

10 The archaeologists found a _____ hidden in the ancient ruins of an underground library.

LESSON FORTY-SEVEN

Target Words

1. Torrid
2. Tortuous
3. Tragedy
4. Tranquil
5. Travesty
6. Trek
7. Trite
8. Truculent
9. Ubiquitous
10. Ultimate

LESSON FORTY-SEVEN

A. Dictation

____ /10

B. Fill in the blanks with the most appropriate words

01 *The Lord of the Rings* follows two Hobbits who _____ to Mordor to destroy a magic ring.

02 His sad attempt to plagiarize my best-selling novel was a _____.

03 Faye has a secret, _____ spot by the creek where she likes to hide away and read.

04 My mom says her dating advice may seem _____, but it's timeworn for a good reason.

05 Jake is historically _____, so I predict it won't be long until he's in anger management again.

06 Smartphones became _____ in the mid-2000s.

07 Their _____ extramarital affair had devastating consequences.

08 The professor held a _____ lecture that left his students completely confounded.

09 My _____ destination is Los Angeles, so it will be a long road trip!

10 Oedipus is the hero of Sophocles' famed _____, *Oedipus Rex*.

LESSON FORTY-EIGHT

Target Words

1. Umbrage
2. Uncanny
3. Undulate
4. Uniform
5. Unilateral
6. Unique
7. Upbraid
8. Vacillate
9. Variance
10. Variegate

LESSON FORTY-EIGHT

A. Dictation

____/10

B. Fill in the blanks with the most appropriate words

01 A famous screenwriting agent quickly bought her _____ film script. He saw the value in her originality!

02 The downtown conservatory has a _____ array of tropical flora and fauna.

03 The dancer began her performance in a tight ball, then _____ each limb with perfect grace.

04 I take _____ at the fact that none of my friends RSVP'd to my party.

05 The laws for adopting a child are not _____ among the states.

06 The tribes and countrymen formed a _____ front. For the first time ever, they were joined as one.

07 I have an _____ knack for knowing when it's about to storm.

08 Certain passages in his new book are at _____ with the philosophy he vociferously touts.

09 Furious, the officer _____ the trainee for disobeying orders.

10 He _____ between the two extremes. For him, there is no moderate position.

LESSON FORTY-NINE

Target Words

1. Vast
2. Veneer
3. Veracious
4. Verbose
5. Vicarious
6. Vicissitudes
7. Vigour (US Vigor)
8. Vim
9. Vivacious
10. Vocation

LESSON FORTY-NINE

A. Dictation

___/10

B. Fill in the blanks with the most appropriate words

01 The astronaut was humbled by the _____ expanse of the galaxy.

02 Her _____ of composure finally cracked under pressure.

03 The knight's strength and _____ had lessened over time.

04 She finds people with philosophy degrees to be quite _____ and opinionated.

05 Todd gleaned _____ pleasure in seeing his enemies fail.

06 He is _____ when it suits him, but his poker face is inscrutable.

07 Unfortunately, we can't foresee every _____ we will face in life.

08 After teaching for over thirty years, the professor had still not lost his _____ for academia.

09 A _____ funk band was a great choice for the wedding reception.

10 Singing is her hobby, but acting is her _____.

LESSON FIFTY

Target Words

1. Volition
2. Voluminous
3. Voluptuary
4. Wane
5. Wax
6. Weary
7. Weather
8. Whet
9. Winsome
10. Zeitgeist

LESSON FIFTY

A. Dictation

____ /10

B. Fill in the blanks with the most appropriate words

01 The TV show *Mad Men* beautifully captures the _____ of the 1960s New York advertising industry.

02 Anna's couture clothes and exorbitant convertible reveal her _____ tendencies.

03 My interest in learning to speak Spanish began to _____ after I left Spain.

04 Hors d'oeuvres are usually served to _____ guests' appetites before a meal is served.

05 Tom and Susan had _____ many storms throughout their twenty-year marriage.

06 Connor's _____ fiancée Donna was a delight at his sister's baby shower.

07 I was _____ and sore after driving in my car for three days straight.

08 Whatever you decide to do, it's ultimately your _____ that matters most.

09 His _____ contributions to the field of biochemistry will not soon be forgotten.

10 The _____ crescent moon will be full in a fortnight.

STAGE
THREE B

LESSON ONE

Target Words

1. Abase
2. Abate
3. Abbreviate
4. Abduct
5. Aberration
6. Abhor
7. Abide
8. Abject
9. Abort
10. Abridge

A. Fill in the blanks with the most appropriate words.

01 I asked him to give me an _____ synopsis of the three-hour movie he had just seen.

02 We will not _____ ourselves by accepting defeat so easily!

03 The outlaw doesn't _____ by the regular rules set upon him by civilized society.

04 I'm sorry my dog bit you. For him, that kind of behaviour is an _____!

05 We will have to _____ our mission due to dangerous technical complications.

06 He offered his most sincere and _____ apology for stealing money from me.

07 We use an _____ for our club name because it has a very long name!

08 The monkeys were _____ from their natural habitat, but help was on the way!

09 Nothing could _____ his terrible, growing rage.

10 I have to admit that I completely _____ the book I just finished reading.

114

LESSON ONE

B. Fill in the blanks in the passage with the most appropriate words.
Passage 1:

Our homework assignment today is to write an _____ synopsis of Shakespeare's play, A Midsummer Night's Dream. My essay is called "Dream: A Study in Folklore." I chose "Dream" because it is an _____ of the title of the play. I loved the play and could not _____ my enthusiasm while writing the essay. You might even say that I _____ my mom and dad from the living room once it was finished and made them read what I had written. They _____ my eagerness because it concerned school. Normally, I _____ working on school projects, but English was my favourite class. Some people may think I _____ myself by being so enthusiastic about something "nerdy" like Shakespeare, but I think that's nonsense! I would publicly declare my adoration of literature, no matter how _____ it may seem! However, those who make fun of me for my love of learning are an _____. Most students I know love to read just as much as I do! We should _____ negative trains of thought that seek to put a damper on enthusiastic learners.

LESSON TWO

Target Words

1. Abrogate
2. Abscond
3. Abundant
4. Accede
5. Accentuate
6. Accommodating
7. Accost
8. Acumen
9. Acute
10. Affable

A. Fill in the blanks with the most appropriate words.

01. The player _____ from the game after seeing his friend waiting for him outside.

02. She has _____ awareness when it comes to style and fashion.

03. He is very generous and _____. He offered to let us stay in his guesthouse!

04. The board of directors voted to _____ the new bill promising annual pay raises.

05. There was _____ evidence to convict the criminal.

06. Roger _____ his son for staying out too late with his friends.

07. These curtains will _____ the colours of the living room carpet.

08. Her _____ and wit make her somewhat intimidating.

09. The roommate _____ to their request that he clean up after himself.

10. Santa Claus is an _____, jolly character who personifies the Christmas spirit.

LESSON TWO

B. Fill in the blanks in the passage with the most appropriate words.
Passage 2:

Recently, Tommy _____ from a secret club, the Monster Team. Normally he is very _____ and loves to look for werewolves and ghosts with the club. However, they recently _____ a deal to only hunt creatures in their small town after hearing about a vampire in Seattle. Tommy would not _____ to the club's request to investigate the matter. He didn't want to be _____ by monsters anymore. Without the club's most reliable and _____ club member to help capture the vampire, they were in trouble. Luckily, there was _____ courage among the other team members. Mike had a great deal of _____ as an investigator, and he was talented with computers. Robin had an _____ sense of hearing and intuition; she was in charge of leading the monster hunts. Regardless, Tommy's absence _____ the fact that they were just a bunch of kids dealing with something dark and dangerous.

LESSON THREE

Target Words

1. Affluent
2. Aggrandize
3. Aggregate
4. Aghast
5. Agoraphobia
6. Akimbo
7. Alacrity
8. Algid
9. Allay
10. Alleviate

A. Fill in the blanks with the most appropriate words.

01. The final act of the play, which ended with the protagonist's death, left the audience _____.

02. Samantha's _____ on the basketball court will win her a scholarship.

03. Unfortunately, his _____ keeps him from having a normal social life.

04. The morning was _____ and foggy. Winter was near.

05. The search party met in the community centre at dusk and _____ their data.

06. This topical cream will help _____ the pain of burns and blisters.

07. She was posed _____ and leaning slightly forward.

08. The politician's _____, privileged upbringing was a hot topic during the campaign.

09. Don't try to _____ my frustration by telling me to calm down!

10. She over-exaggerated the facts of the story to _____ her own actions.

LESSON THREE

B. Fill in the blanks in the passage with the most appropriate words.
Passage 3:

Joseph used to have _____ but was able to overcome it thanks to the help of a therapist. His friend Tim, who had terrible anxiety, _____ the therapist by claiming he had been totally cured. Tim, however, was from an _____ neighborhood, so Joseph was not sure he could afford the therapist. Luckily, his health insurance would _____ the cost of each session. It was on an _____ Tuesday morning that Joseph had his first appointment with the therapist. Dr. Keenan had agreed to come to Joseph's house. Joseph stood _____ in his living room, too nervous to sit, as he waited for the doctor to arrive. Finally, there was a knock on the door. Dr. Keenan had finally come! First, Dr. Keenan asked Joseph to tell him about his condition. Joseph explained he used to be a happy, fearless young man with the _____ of a teenager. However, after getting into a car accident, Joseph's anxiety was never fully _____. Dr. Keenan told Joseph to _____ all of his painful memories and channel them into a healthy hobby, like running. Joseph was _____. He had never considered something so simple. He bought a treadmill, and steadily began running every day. After a month, he even went on a run outside, around his entire neighborhood!

LESSON FOUR

Target Words

1. Aloof
2. Altercation
3. Amalgamation
4. Ambivalent
5. Amble
6. Ameliorate
7. Amend
8. Amiable
9. Amourous (US Amorous)
10. Amorphous

A. Fill in the blanks with the most appropriate words.

01 Many people feel _____ and romantic on Valentine's Day.

02 The police officer tried to _____ the situation by arresting people, but it only made it worse!

03 The book is an _____ of many different literary themes.

04 I was _____ about being accepted into the university. Was that school the right fit for me?

05 She _____ over to me from the bus station and begged for spare change.

06 Her parents went through an unpleasant divorce, but they have since made _____.

07 The comedian seemed quite _____ on stage, but he was ill-mannered in person.

08 The philosophy professor is very _____. He is always caught up in his own world.

09 Becca had an _____ with the restaurant manager after finding human hair in her food!

10 The _____ and indefinite nature of politics can be overwhelming.

LESSON FOUR

B. Fill in the blanks in the passage with the most appropriate words.
Passage 4:

When I first met Kyle, he was an _____ young man who had no friends. He seemed _____ when it came to school; he wasn't rude to his classmates, but he wasn't _____ either. He rarely caused _____ because he spent so much time by himself. He would _____ through the hallways, going from class to class, rarely speaking to anyone. But all of that changed when Clara transferred to his school. Kyle was drawn to Clara from the start. She could _____ any class discussion by contributing her original opinions and ideas. A number of _____ boys in Kyle's grade asked Clara out on dates, but Clara denied them all. There was an inexplicably _____ charm about her that Kyle didn't quite understand. She seemed to be an _____ of every good quality that existed in a person! She was kind, honest, curious, and non-judgmental. Kyle made a conscious effort to _____ his antisocial behaviour and asked if Clara wanted to be his friend. To his joy and surprise, Clara said nothing would make her happier!

LESSON FIVE

Target Words

1. Anomaly
2. Antechamber
3. Anxiety
4. Aphorism
5. Apocalypse
6. Apparitional
7. Arbitrator
8. Ascetic
9. Assuage
10. Atone (for)

A. Fill in the blanks with the most appropriate words.

01 Daniel has always been _____. He goes to church every day.

02 He _____ my frustration by offering to compromise.

03 The slow-moving fog creeping over the mountains is an _____ sight.

04 I sat in the _____, waiting for the receptionist to call my name.

05 My _____ gets much worse if I neglect to take my medicine.

06 The pious man _____ for his sins by going to confession bi-weekly.

07 People think the polar lights are an _____ of nature, but they actually occur multiple times a year!

08 There was an _____ present during the investigation to make sure things remained civil.

09 My neighbours are stockpiling groceries like the _____ is coming!

10 His most common _____ is, "If it ain't broke, don't fix it."

LESSON FIVE

B. Fill in the blanks in the passage with the most appropriate words.
Passage 5:

I had been chosen to test a new drug that was said to cure cancer. My _____ about testing a potentially dangerous substance was _____ when I learned that there had already been a successful test run of the drug. Still, the company worried their first test group had been a medical _____, so they conducted a second test to be sure the drug was safe. My group contained four other people. One of the other test subjects was an _____ who hadn't gone to chemotherapy in almost a month. He looked sickly, almost _____, in that he was pale and fragile as glass. Another of the test subjects was an aging woman who considered her newfound breast cancer a means of _____ for her past mistakes. The third test subject was a high-strung young man with stage 3 cancer, who believed the _____ was near. The four of us sat in the _____ until the doctor called our names. While I waited, I thought about an _____ I had heard my grandma once say: "All good thing comes to those who wait." However, I wondered: would the cancer drug I was waiting to test be a success or a failure? The next few months would serve as the _____.

123

LESSON SIX

Target Words

1. Audacious
2. Augment
3. Austere
4. Baleful
5. Bard
6. Battery
7. Belligerent
8. Benevolent
9. Benign
10. Berate

A. Fill in the blanks with the most appropriate words.

01 I _____ my summer allowance by mowing lawns for the neighbours.

02 The principal is a _____ woman who has a lot of love and compassion for her students.

03 Her face was calm and _____ as she told me she loved me.

04 I will _____ every single person who litters!

05 The team captain shot the referee a _____ look and then angrily took a seat on the sidelines.

06 Your _____ and unruly behaviour during class has earned you detention!

07 My _____ brother starts fights whenever he sees an opportunity.

08 Many of Shakespeare's plays feature _____ and long soliloquies.

09 _____ is a serious offence. It can put you behind bars.

10 The winter forest, devoid of leaves and life, was cold and _____.

LESSON SIX

B. Fill in the blanks in the passage with the most appropriate words.
Passage 6:

Recently, my math professor Mr. Banks _____ me for not doing my homework. He is a _____ teacher who truly cares about whether or not his students are learning. Therefore, he asked me to stay after class one day. I was expecting an _____ conversation about how I needed to try harder, but Mr. Banks surprised me. He asked me if everything was ok. With a _____ expression, he explained how he knew sometimes difficulties at home could lead to difficulties with schoolwork. Being somewhat _____ in nature, I grew defensive and insisted nothing was wrong. Mr. Banks saw through my _____ attempt to lie my way out of this uncomfortable situation. He knew something was wrong. Finally, I broke down and admitted my parents had been fighting a lot. I had caught my parents' _____ glances at one another over breakfast, and their heated arguments at dinner. Luckily, neither of them had committed something as terrible as _____. Regardless, their attempt to hide their fights from me only _____ the tension and aggravated the whole situation. I was resentful that they could not talk to me about their problems like reasonable adults. Mr. Banks gave me an extra week to complete my homework, and from then on, he and I talked once a week. He was like a _____ of wisdom and compassion during that difficult time, offering me the empathy and attention I couldn't find at home.

LESSON SEVEN

Target Words

1. Bereft
2. Bide
3. Bilk
4. Blandish
5. Bloated
6. Boisterous
7. Bourgeois
8. Brash
9. Brazen
10. Brumal

A. Fill in the blanks with the most appropriate words.

01. The renter _____ their landlord by purposely underpaying the rent, so they were issued a warning.

02. After being pulled over, Meg _____ the police officer, hoping she would get out of a ticket.

03. Your friend is too _____. He always hurts people's feelings, even if he doesn't mean to.

04. January is usually _____ here in Vancouver. It snows sometimes too!

05. My stomach felt _____ after I ate too much over Thanksgiving break.

06. The child was acting too _____, so the mother took him outside.

07. Tina is fearless and daring, but sometimes she can be too _____.

08. _____ of any patience, the man started yelling at the people in line ahead of him.

09. He described Basquiat's artwork as _____, a haunting depiction of the proletariat.

10. Until my brother showed up, I would _____ my time in a bookstore.

LESSON SEVEN

B. Fill in the blanks in the passage with the most appropriate words.
Passage 7:

It was a _____ morning, and frost covered the lawns. Tyler biked through his _____ neighbourhood, gazing at each modest house as he went by. He passed old Mr. Boris's house. Mr. Boris was a _____ older man who frightened the children with his aggressive shouting. Tyler's mom said Mr. Boris wasn't rude. She claimed he was just a _____ gentleman who wouldn't put up with mischievous children running around on his lawn and ruining his flowerbeds. Mr. Boris was sitting on his porch that morning when Tyler went up to his door. Mr. Boris was a bit overweight, with a round, _____ stomach on which his hands rested as he sat in a rocking chair. His eyes narrowed as Tyler neared. Tyler _____ his time as he walked up to the porch. Mr. Boris made him nervous. He doubted he could _____ the old man out of anything, much less a friendly exchange. Nonetheless, Mr. Boris greeted Tyler with a _____ greeting, which startled Tyler. Tyler took out a newspaper and handed it to Mr. Boris. He considered _____ Mr. Boris with small talk to get on Mr. Boris's side. However, Tyler had a feeling Mr. Boris would see right through this ruse. Though _____ of his youth, Mr. Boris was a sharp, observant man. Tyler gave him the newspaper, said goodbye, and pedaled off on his bike as fast as he could.

LESSON EIGHT

Target Words

1. Brusque
2. Buffet (n.)
3. Buffet (vt.)
4. Burgeon
5. Cacophony
6. Cadence
7. Cajole
8. Callous
9. Calumny
10. Camaraderie

A. Fill in the blanks with the most appropriate words.

01 The corrupt company _____ its new employees into signing away their vacation days.

02 The small, local band _____ into a nationally recognized rock-and-roll group.

03 Her _____ response to his love letter sent Ryan into a pit of despair.

04 My friends are coming over for dinner. I have prepared an enormous _____.

05 The rough seas _____ the coast, battering the cliffside with angry waves.

06 His boss's _____ reply to the email made him nervous. Was he about to be fired?

07 The song has a slow _____ that picks up speed after the second chorus.

08 The club prides itself on its ability to foster _____ among total strangers.

09 _____, or slander, is a serious offence that people take seriously.

10 There are four preschools around the corner, so there is a _____ of screaming kids all day.

LESSON EIGHT

B. Fill in the blanks in the passage with the most appropriate words.
Passage 8:

Recently I _____ my friend Kate into going to a music show with me. The band was _____ into a very popular musical group. The band had come into the limelight recently after a journalist had made them the target of _____. The journalist had claimed their music was for devil-worshippers! The article had initially been a _____ against the band that had hurt their reputation, but soon they had a dedicated fan base that prided themselves on acceptance, togetherness, and _____. The band's _____ reply to the article had come in the form of a song titled, "What Do They Know?" The song's _____ and hypnotic guitar patterns always got people dancing at their shows. Their concerts were a _____ of cheering fans, clapping hands, and exciting music. Kate could be quite _____ when it came to music, and rarely showed enthusiasm for new things, but she admitted after the show that she had had a great time. We were tired and hungry, so we stopped at a _____-style restaurant to eat our weight in Mexican food.

LESSON NINE

Target Words

1. Canvas
2. Capricious
3. Captivate
4. Carouse
5. Cavity
6. Cavort
7. Celestial
8. Chastise
9. Choreographed
10. Circumlocution

A. Fill in the blanks with the most appropriate words.

01. The judge's vague _____ made the verdict confusing.

02. We danced and _____ until the sun came up.

03. Under a microscope we can see that the surface of this plant is marked by ridges and _____.

04. The happy cats chased each other's tails and _____ across the garden.

05. Astronomy is the study of _____ bodies.

06. My mom will _____ me if I don't finish my homework before dinner.

07. The book _____ me from the very start. I couldn't put it down!

08. As a photographer, the world is my _____. I do not need paintbrushes; I only need my camera.

09. My friend helped _____ our high school's production of *Little Shop of Horrors*.

10. Being _____ isn't always a good thing. Sometimes it's better to be consistent.

LESSON NINE

B. Fill in the blanks in the passage with the most appropriate words.
Passage 9:

There are many different kinds of artist. Some use _____ dance to depict stories or emotions. Others create paintings on _____, and use colour and light to create striking scenes. Eleanor is a photographer who takes pictures of the night sky. She is fascinated by all things _____ and has spent countless hours staring at the stars. As a child, she was _____ by her parents for spending too much time outside. However, she now gets paid for her work! She is constantly _____ by the wonders of the heavens, and sometimes her hobby can lead her to be quite _____. In the past she has impulsively bought plane tickets to view sights like the Milky Way galaxy from a pitch-dark national park; once she even went to a Northern Lights festival in Iceland and spent a night _____ with locals and celebrating the natural beauty of the earth. They _____ across the snowy plains, and Eleanor would take countless pictures of the beautiful, joyful scene. Whenever she tried to explain why she loved studying the heavens, she found her _____ fell short. She could never find the right words to explain it, but one thing she knew for sure: art filled a spiritual _____ deep inside her soul, and for that she was grateful.

LESSON TEN

Target Words

1. Circumspect
2. Clairvoyant
3. Claustrophobia
4. Cliché
5. Coalesce
6. Cogent
7. Collusion
8. Colossus
9. Comatose
10. Commendable

A. Fill in the blanks with the most appropriate words.

01 The bridge was weathered away in places, so I was _____ when I crossed it.

02 The way she so bravely sticks up for her morals is _____.

03 His _____ defense of his thesis earned him high marks.

04 We were concerned their _____ would have dangerous consequences.

05 The London Eye is a _____ in the centre of the city. The Ferris wheel is 135 meters tall!

06 The writing professor was sick of reading the same timeworn _____ in his students' papers.

07 My cousin Elaine tells fortunes and reads palms. She is a gifted _____.

08 After heavy rainfall, the streams _____ into one big river.

09 Playing soccer all day left me feeling all but _____. I needed to rest.

10 My _____ prevents me from venturing into very small spaces.

LESSON TEN

B. Fill in the blanks in the passage with the most appropriate words.

Passage 10:

_____ is, in my opinion, a debilitating disease of the mind. It prevents me from doing mundane things like taking an elevator or walking through tunnels. Sometimes it leaves me nearly _____ with fear, and I am left in a catatonic state of terror. Other times, my fear and anxiety _____ to become paranoia. I've always been _____ about the idea of seeking professional therapy, but my friend mentioned that with the help of a talented psychiatrist, she had gotten over her fear of flying. She remarked that the doctor had been almost _____ in his ability to detect the source of her phobia. I thought it was _____ that she had conquered her fear, so I made an appointment with him. The office was located in a _____ of a building that towered above the other skyscrapers downtown. Luckily, his office was on the third floor, so there was no need for me to take the elevator! The psychiatrist's name was Dr. O'Malley. He was a _____ and articulate man in his late forties who listened carefully as I described my fear of small spaces. At the end of our meeting, he gave me an assignment: take the elevator down to the lobby. It was only three floors! I surprised myself by completing this assignment. Maybe the age-old _____ was true: what doesn't kill you only makes you stronger!

LESSON ELEVEN

Target Words

1. Commodious
2. Compel
3. Complicit
4. Compliment
5. Concede
6. Conciliatory
7. Concoct
8. Concord
9. Conduit
10. Confluence

A. Fill in the blanks with the most appropriate words.

01 The underground _____ that connects our two towns collapsed after a tornado tore through it.

02 The creative _____ of the art, music and drama departments led to an amazing school musical that everyone would remember for years.

03 I denied being _____ in the cruel senior prank on our high school principal.

04 The local council meetings are frustrating and tedious because they rarely end in progress or _____.

05 We _____ to the harsh truth: despite how long and hard we had tried, we had still lost the race.

06 Sara has the most _____ room of all the siblings because she is the oldest.

07 Dr. Reed couldn't _____ his patient to quit smoking, but he pleaded with him nonetheless.

08 My teacher _____ my English essay and gave me the best grade in class!

09 Who _____ this incredible meal? I need to tell them how delicious it was!

10 We ended the meeting on a _____ note and left the boardroom with smiles on our faces.

LESSON ELEVEN

B. Fill in the blanks in the passage with the most appropriate words.
Passage 11:

Reunions are a great way for a _____ of people to reconnect with both close and long-distance friends. Recently my grandparents _____ a plan to reunite members of our family that hadn't seen each other for years. Aunt Greta acted as a _____ for our long-distance relatives because she was good at staying in touch with people, despite not seeing them for years. We all _____ to a date, and my grandparents rented a _____ event space in Vancouver where we could all meet. My mom _____ my sisters and me to dress nicely for the family reunion, so we all put on our best shoes and dresses. Later, my grandparents would _____ us on being the best-dressed girls at the party. Once everyone had arrived, we played a few games like musical chairs and charades. It was a _____ affair, and everyone was so happy to have had the chance to reconnect after so much time apart. After some discussion, we reached a _____ and agreed to have annual family reunions. Unfortunately, my Uncle Taz, who was later found to be _____ in an act of embezzlement, would not be around next year to attend the family reunion…

LESSON TWELVE

Target Words

1. Confound
2. Connotation
3. Contusion
4. Convalescence
5. Copious
6. Corpulent
7. Cosmopolitan
8. Credulity
9. Cursory
10. Daft

A. Fill in the blanks with the most appropriate words.

01 His refusal to admit any wrongdoing deeply _____ me because he was obviously guilty!

02 My _____ has landed me in a few embarrassing situations. I used to believe that swallowing watermelon seeds would cause a watermelon to grow in my stomach!

03 She had a _____ amount to eat over Thanksgiving break, so it's no wonder she gained five pounds in just three days!

04 The nurses celebrated my mom's _____. She had been doing physical therapy for six months and was finally able to walk again!

05 My somewhat _____ friend decided to start exercising more often.

06 Sometimes I get _____ on my legs, and I don't remember how I got them!

07 My most _____ friend has been to over twenty different countries.

08 The professor gets annoyed when someone asks a _____ question that's been answered in a previous lecture, but she reminds herself that it's part of the job.

09 *Citizen Kane* is a film that explores the _____ of fame and fortune.

10 He gave me a _____ farewell that proved he wouldn't miss me at all while he was gone.

LESSON TWELVE

B. Fill in the blanks in the passage with the most appropriate words.
Passage 12:

Tony had always been _____, from childhood through adolescence to adulthood, and he was sick of being overweight. There were many negative _____ of the word "fat," but Tony knew there were major health concerns to consider as well. Eating _____ amounts of food at every meal had become a habit, and it was one Tony hoped to kick. At first, his _____ about so-called "fad diets" had sent him spiraling down a rabbit-hole of futile food and fitness regiments that yielded _____ results. It seemed like he would never shed the weight. However, one of Tony's brothers, a _____ young man who spent much of his time in the gym, suggested he hire a personal trainer. At first, Tony thought the suggestion was _____. After all, how could a personal trainer help Tony in a way that Tony couldn't do himself? Nonetheless, he soon warmed to the idea. He hoped a physical trainer would guide him through his journey to _____. He hated to admit that he was obese, but it was hard to ignore the harmful physical consequences of being so overweight. At first, he figured the personal trainer would give Tony a _____ glance and decide his case was hopeless. That would be an emotional _____ too painful to bear. However, the physical trainer confided in Tony that he too had once been very overweight, and that shedding the weight had simply been a matter of dedication and self-discipline. Finally, Tony felt confident that he was on the path to a healthier life.

LESSON THIRTEEN

Target Words

1. Daunting
2. Dearth
3. Defame
4. Deft
5. Defunct
6. Deleterious
7. Delude
8. Deluge
9. Derelict
10. Desolate

A. Fill in the blanks with the most appropriate words.

01. The preacher _____ his congregation, promising they would go to heaven if they gave him money.

02. There is a _____ of passion in our university's uninspired Math Department.

03. The book was considered _____ because it promoted supposedly dangerous ideas.

04. A contrived confession served to _____ the senator. No one could support him any longer.

05. The house has become _____ and uninhabitable without anyone there to maintain it.

06. Running a full marathon is a _____ task, especially for those who have never done it before!

07. He is _____ with computers and was promoted to manager at the tech repair store in no time.

08. After the bomb, the burned-down forest had become barren and _____.

09. The dam burst, and the ensuing _____ left the town in ruins.

10. In its prime, the now-_____ newspaper provided news to thousands of people each day.

LESSON THIRTEEN

B. Fill in the blanks in the passage with the most appropriate words.
Passage 13:

The old dam was _____, but no one knew how important it was until too late. For weeks, the news had covered a _____ report about an incoming storm of biblical proportions. The town of Hayberry was expected a _____ of rain. The mayor went on TV and unknowingly _____ the citizens by claiming the city was prepared for the worst. He went on to assure everyone that their _____ and practiced emergency teams were prepared for such _____ events including hailstorms, tornadoes, and floods. The mayor was even so confident that he said he expected a _____ of rain on the predicted day of the storm--that it would only be a light sprinkling of rain instead of a downpour. Still, the town became _____ as the storm grew near. People were leaving in droves. Schools, churches, and office buildings became temporarily _____ as everyone fled for higher ground. On the day of the storm, almost no one was in town, which was fortunate because the dam burst, and the town was flooded with nearly eight feet of water. The mayor was _____ for his carefree attitude preceding the storm. Afterwards, he was horrified that he had been so blasé about it. Dozens of homes were destroyed in the wake of the flood.

LESSON FOURTEEN

Target Words

1. Despondent
2. Destitute
3. Diaphanous
4. Dictate
5. Differentiate
6. Dilapidated
7. Diligent
8. Diminish
9. Diminutive
10. Discreet

A. Fill in the blanks with the most appropriate words.

01. It's hard to _____ between truth and lies when you fabricate everything!

02. We became _____ after the stock market crash.

03. Don't let the rude comments of a failed competitor _____ your victory.

04. During the test, the teacher caught a student _____ pulling out a cheat sheet.

05. I felt _____ after being fired from my job and then getting dumped by my girlfriend.

06. He is a _____ musician who practices guitar every day for two hours.

07. The fabric of her dress is _____. It is sheer and iridescent in the light.

08. He _____ a rule that anyone who was late would have to stand for the remainder of the class.

09. The _____ dancer is very waifish, though she can be very graceful.

10. Having been abandoned for nearly fifteen years, the library was quite _____.

LESSON FOURTEEN

B. Fill in the blanks in the passage with the most appropriate words.
Passage 14:

I have astronomy class in the _____ top-floor lecture room of a bright, airy tower on campus. My professor seemed _____ and aloof at first, but soon I found that he was just an odd fellow. Though he could appear solemn and pensive at times, he ended up being one of the most _____ professors I've ever known. During the first class, he made sure to _____ between the study of astronomy and astrology. He _____ that we would only be learning astronomy in his class because he viewed astrology as a non-scientific hoax. I _____ heard someone whisper that they had hoped this class would be about astrology, and consequently I did not see that person again after that! The astronomy tower had once been a _____ building on campus, but after my professor was hired, he was put in charge of the entire department. Granted, the department was small and somewhat _____, being starved of much school funding. However, these hurdles didn't _____ his hope and vision for the Astronomy Department. Within three years, it had gone from being a _____ program with two professors and fifteen students total to being one of the most popular programs offered at the university!

LESSON FIFTEEN

Target Words

1. Discrete
2. Disparage
3. Dissonance
4. Divergent
5. Diverse
6. Divisive
7. Domicile
8. Doppelgänger
9. Douse
10. Dutiful

A. Fill in the blanks with the most appropriate words.

01. _____ between the jurors led to a seven-hour deliberation.

02. The new Broadway play boasts a _____ cast of people with different backgrounds and ethnicities.

03. _____ interpretations of my artwork led me to reconsider my thematic intentions.

04. He crafted a _____ scheme that would tear the teammates apart from the inside.

05. The robber admitted he had broken into hundreds of _____ and shops during the worst of his criminal years.

06. She _____ the couch in lighter fluid and then set it on fire.

07. We try to be _____ at work by lending a helping hand wherever it's needed.

08. Some people say my celebrity _____ is Cate Blanchett, but I think they're just flattering me.

09. The cruel king never missed an opportunity to _____ his lowliest subjects. He found pleasure in humiliating even the most pitiful people in his kingdom.

10. Critics' _____ opinions concerning the documentary led to some debate over whether it had any artistic value.

LESSON FIFTEEN

B. Fill in the blanks in the passage with the most appropriate words.
Passage 15:

There was much _____ in the land about whether King Henry was fit to rule. He had proved himself to be a _____ sort of king, and in the worst way, in that he ruled much more harshly than those before him. Even his _____ staff of knights, lords, squires, and maids agreed that he was a menace. Something had to be done. People hid in their _____ when the king paraded through town, terrified that he might unleash his cruelty upon them. Once, he had ordered his guards to _____ a farmer's crops with brine simply because the farmer would not let the king buy his beautiful young daughter as his house slave. The king's most _____ adviser finally agreed something had to be done when the king ordered the ruthless murder of a poor family merely because the family was from a foreign city. Their salvation came in the form of a young man that came to town one day who was almost identical to the king. A _____ coup was planned. The guards, knowing the wellbeing of all citizens was in jeopardy, killed the king and had the _____ take his place. Unfortunately, the twin was even more terrible than the king he had replaced because he wanted his own _____ identity! It was a _____ lesson indeed.

LESSON SIXTEEN

Target Words

1. Dynamic
2. Elocution
3. Elucidate
4. Empathetic
5. Empathy
6. Enervate
7. Enervated
8. Entity
9. Entomology
10. Envious

A. Fill in the blanks with the most appropriate words.

01. Gina couldn't help but feel _____ of her friend's success when she had tried just as hard to accomplish the same goals.

02. I need to get over my fear of _____ before I give my bridesmaid's speech at the wedding.

03. The stock market is a _____ economic beast that is always changing, for better or for worse.

04. Her lack of _____ makes her a callous and uncompromising person.

05. I went for a long run and then ate a big meal, so now I feel _____.

06. _____ is not for me. I think cockroaches, spiders, and wasps are creepy!

07. The graduate student's thesis would _____ abstract theories concerning anti-matter in space.

08. The church and the police force had come together to form a powerful but dangerous _____.

09. I am very _____ towards animals, so it should be no surprise that I'm vegetarian!

10. Staying up all night to study for the big test had _____ me.

LESSON SIXTEEN

B. Fill in the blanks in the passage with the most appropriate words.
Passage 16:

My sister Beth is moving into her dorm at the university today. I am very _____ that she gets to go to such a nice university, while I am still in high school. I tried to feel happy for her and put myself in her shoes, but _____ doesn't always come easily to me. My family and I were _____ after helping her move into her dorm that day. Beth's roommate was already there. She is a talkative young woman named Meg whose _____ and endless conversation wore us all out. Already I started to feel _____ towards my sister, who would have to deal with Meg's constant chattering for the next year! Beth would be _____ by Meg's high energy by the end of the semester, without a doubt! I wondered if she might request a change of roommates if it got to be too much. Over lunch we discussed what Beth would study at the university. Her academic interests are quite _____, so she has yet to decide her major. The waiter put our food down, and suddenly a roach crawled out from under my plate! Beth waved it away and laughed. I said maybe she should study _____ if she's so fearless when it comes to bugs. She said she wasn't interested in creepy-crawlies or any _____ that belonged in the dirt. I asked her to _____ what she meant, but she just said it was getting late, and to hurry and eat my sandwich.

LESSON SEVENTEEN

Target Words

1. Erect
2. Erroneous
3. Espouse
4. Espy
5. Ethereal
6. Euphoric
7. Exacerbate
8. Excursion
9. Exemplary
10. Exigent

A. Fill in the blanks with the most appropriate words.

01 A new luxury apartment complex was _____. It would house the most affluent citizens.

02 I turned away from the radical ideas I had _____ in my youth.

03 It was an _____ matter that required the policeman's immediate attention.

04 She knew him well and easily _____ the falsehood glimmering behind his eyes.

05 We took an _____ into the mountains for a picnic on the peaks.

06 The award-winning documentary was an _____ look into the lives of deep-sea divers.

07 My _____ impression of him misled me to believe he was a nice person.

08 The runner was _____ after he won the race for which he had trained for seven months.

09 Facing arrest, the illegal street performer _____ the situation by yelling at anyone who looked at him.

10 The stained glass windows give the living room an _____ glow.

LESSON SEVENTEEN

B. Fill in the blanks in the passage with the most appropriate words.
Passage 17:

My current house was _____ in 1920. Needless to say, it has some issues. I made some _____ assumptions when I first bought the house—mainly that it wouldn't need to be fixed. Unfortunately, I _____ many issues with the house during my first year living there. Though it is a beautiful house with _____ stained glass windows and a gorgeous spiral staircase, I was less than _____ to learn that the building had more "character" than I bargained for. For example, there was black mould growing in the basement! This was an _____ issue that I had to fix immediately, because black mold could be deadly. Luckily, this could be taken care of within a month or two, but what happened next was totally unpredictable. I took a weekend _____ to my parents' house in Atlanta, and when I came back, I found the roof was leaking in multiple places! Apparently, the roof wasn't in great condition to start with, so bad weather only _____ the issue. My parents _____ the belief I should move out when I learned that it would cost thousands of dollars to fix everything. Sadly, it just wasn't worth it! The house may have looked _____ on the outside, but on the inside, it was far from perfect.

LESSON EIGHTEEN

Target Words

1. Existential
2. Exorbitant
3. Extol
4. Extravagant
5. Fabricate
6. Fabulist
7. Facile
8. Fallacious
9. Familial
10. Fatuous

A. Fill in the blanks with the most appropriate words.

01. It was a _____ task, simple enough to be completed within the hour.

02. I _____ him for participating in the marathon fundraiser, which was a huge success.

03. Our teacher doesn't appreciate _____ behaviour and will happily hand out demerits to misbehaving students.

04. My grandpa George is a bit of a _____, but he means well.

05. Cloe's sixteenth birthday party was _____. She got a brand new BMW, and all her friends received $15 gift cards for Starbucks!

06. A _____ emergency called me out of town. My brother was in a skiing accident.

07. She was having an _____ crisis and didn't know what she wanted to do with her life.

08. The criminal _____ his alibi, but the police officers had proof that he was lying.

09. Her _____ assumption about the outcome of the debate led to some embarrassment.

10. The _____ rise in rent in our city cannot be blamed on one single factor.

LESSON EIGHTEEN

B. Fill in the blanks in the passage with the most appropriate words.

Passage 18:

No one was more excited for the _____ party than Theo. She was given the task of making and sending out invitations. Initially, she thought this job would be _____ and that she could complete it within a day. However, the guest list was _____, including over 300 names. Theo had been hired by the curators of the party, an older couple named Steven and Margo. Their _____ assumption that the invitations would only take a few days to make had frustrated Theo. She calmly explained that even with her staff of four other employees, it would take at least three weeks to assemble the invitations. Luckily, Theo's employees were hard workers, and she felt a _____ kinship with them. Later she _____ them for putting extra time into this project simply to please their _____ and somewhat naïve customers. Steven, the husband, was a bit of a _____ and told his wife Margo that he had already paid for all 350 custom-made invitations. Margo learned this claim was an obvious _____. However, when she received the bill for the invitations, it was over $500! She nearly had an _____ breakdown as she wondered how invitations could cost so much. But when she got her own invitation in the mail, she realized that Theo and her staff were incredibly talented. The invitations were exquisite! It was all anyone could talk about at the party!

LESSON NINETEEN

Target Words

1. Fecund
2. Feign
3. Feral
4. Fetter
5. Fey
6. Fickle
7. Figurative
8. Firmament
9. Flabbergasted
10. Flaccid

A. Fill in the blanks with the most appropriate words.

01 The _____ above us glittered like diamonds in the night sky.

02 There is a hard-to-describe, _____ quality about her smile. It's like she knows all your secrets.

03 The zoo's new panda is a _____ female that had twin babies this year!

04 I accidentally ruined the surprise party for Ben, but he _____ shock anyway.

05 School had left me _____ with so much responsibility and homework.

06 I shook his limp and _____ hand, which instantly repulsed me.

07 Some think the term "the grass is always greener on the other side" is _____, but as far as my horticulturist neighbors go, it's very literal!

08 Raccoons may be cute, but they are also _____, so don't try to pet them!

09 The end of the horror movie _____ me. None of the characters survived!

10 The weather here can be _____. One day it's freezing cold, and the next it's sweltering hot!

LESSON NINETEEN

B. Fill in the blanks in the passage with the most appropriate words.
Passage 19:

It was a cold day, but Susan and Laurie weren't prepared for such frigid weather. The weather had been _____ lately; it was hard to plan an outfit for the day because they never knew if it would be hot or cold, or rainy or sunny. Despite the cold, Susan and Laurie went to a botanical garden together. The garden was on two _____ acres of lush land, and there were many different seasonal plants and flowers to observe. Laurie was worried the cold would _____ their efforts to stay very long. However, soon it warmed enough that they felt comfortable walking around without wearing their hats, scarves, and gloves. They made their way to the rose garden, where both young women were _____ by the beauty of the roses. They had not wilted or gone _____ from the cold; in fact, they seemed to be enjoying the frost on their petals! The garden was magical--so _____ and rich with colour. Susan was delighted by a small squirrel, which scurried out from under a bush and ran across the path. She wanted to pet it, but Laurie reminded her that it was a _____ creature unaccustomed to human affection. The sky soon grew dark, and day turned to twilight. Stars were beginning to glimmer in the darkening _____ above, so Susan and Laurie headed towards the exit. Laurie _____ reluctance to leave; in fact, she was hungry and was very much ready to go home! However, she didn't want to be a wet blanket, which was a _____ phrase she had heard before. Being a wet blanket meant you put a damper on a good time. Laurie was not that type of person, so she reluctantly acted cheerful all the way home.

LESSON TWENTY

Target Words

1. Flattery
2. Flout
3. Fluctuate
4. Flux
5. Forage
6. Forestall
7. Forlorn
8. Formidable
9. Forsake
10. Fortify

A. Fill in the blanks with the most appropriate words.

01. Some say imitation is a form of _____; if your friend is copying your style, take it as a compliment!

02. The crow dug its beak into the dirt, _____ for worms or leftover crumbs of food.

03. I tried to _____ the inevitable, but it was indeed inevitable.

04. The film follows a _____ violinist who loses his job and has to declare bankruptcy.

05. My opinion on the matter _____. Sometimes I am in favour, other times I am opposed.

06. He is a _____ opponent, but I tried not to feel intimidated.

07. During rush hour, there is a _____ of people leaving work to go home.

08. She _____ the rule that forbade cigarettes at school, and promptly earned detention.

09. The military base camp was _____ with barriers and weapons in case of attack.

10. No one should _____ their family.

LESSON TWENTY

B. Fill in the blanks in the passage with the most appropriate words.
Passage 20:

Though they had _____ the house against intruders, Mason and Chloe were worried it wouldn't be enough. The _____ armed robbers outside their house were eager to get in. Mason decided they should try to _____ the robbers by creating a diversion, then making a run for it. Their car was in the driveway, but Mason would have to _____ through the house in search of the keys. Plus, once he found the keys, there was no guarantee the car would start. The vehicle had been _____ in terms of reliability; some days the engine wouldn't start at all! When he relayed this information to Chloe, she became _____. She wondered if they should just let the robbers in and pray they didn't hurt them. Perhaps she could use charm and _____ on the robbers in an attempt to sweet-talk them out of robbing them. Or maybe, while the robbers were rooting through their things, Mason and Chloe would be _____ and then have a chance to slip away unnoticed. Luckily, Mason found an old cell phone in the attic that, remarkably, still held a charge. He dialed 911 and told the operator about the burglars outside their house who were ready to _____ the laws of armed robbery. Within ten minutes, a _____ of police officers arrived at their house to rescue Mason and Chloe.

LESSON TWENTY-ONE

Target Words

1. Fortitude
2. Fortuitous
3. Foster
4. Frenetic
5. Gape
6. Gay
7. Gluttonous
8. Goad
9. Gourmand
10. Grandiose

A. Fill in the blanks with the most appropriate words.

01 I don't consider myself a _____ because I eat out of necessity and not enjoyment.

02 A teacher's duty is to _____ a safe and supportive learning environment.

03 During Thanksgiving, I can be quite _____. Last year I gained five pounds in just two days!

04 Our _____ dogs couldn't contain their excitement about seeing us after we were gone for a week.

05 The awe-struck spectators _____ at the Olympic gymnast, who had just broken numerous records.

06 I _____ Tommy into joining us on our camping trip because he seemed lonely.

07 She prides herself on her _____. She is a courageous and resilient young woman.

08 The wedding was _____. The family spent close to a million dollars on the decadent event.

09 The similarities between her book and Stephen King's are not _____. I suspect plagiarism.

10 The musicians arrived and began to strike up the lively harps, joyful drums and _____ flutes.

LESSON TWENTY-ONE

B. Fill in the blanks in the passage with the most appropriate words.
Passage 21:

Some people don't understand what a _____ is. This can be confused with a _____ person, but they are not the same thing. One enjoys food, while the other cannot get enough of it. My Aunt Liza has become a bit of a glutton. Last Christmas I couldn't help but _____ at her as she piled her dinner plate with enough to feed three adults! Her appetite is quite _____. She happens to weigh three hundred pounds, so her eating habits are obviously affecting her health. My mom, Aunt Liza's sister, tried to _____ her into eating less, but Aunt Liza was very offended by the suggestion. She became _____ with anger and refused to hear another word. Still, her appetite needed to change, or else she could be in serious trouble. It takes _____ and self-awareness to admit you need help, but Aunt Liza just wouldn't seek any. However, by some _____ stroke of luck, she developed a crush on a friend from work. She wanted to impress that friend, so she started eating less. She even started going to a gym, which is a great place to lose weight because it _____ a healthy living style. Within a few months, she had lost seventy pounds, and she was back to being the _____, carefree, and healthy Aunt Liza we all knew and loved.

LESSON TWENTY-TWO

Target Words

1. Gregarious
2. Grotto
3. Guile
4. Hail
5. Hapless
6. Harmony
7. Harrowing
8. Hedonist
9. Henchman
10. Hiatus

A. Fill in the blanks with the most appropriate words.

01 I became more _____ after I started paying more attention to my social health and meeting new people.

02 Be careful around Maxine. She may seem nice, but that's only to distract you from her _____ and scheming nature.

03 The trail led us to a creek, which in turn led us to a _____. It was so dark and menacing that we turned back immediately.

04 I wish you wouldn't be such a _____. You should try to practice some self-discipline!

05 The _____ customer suffered a duplicitous and disastrous deal made by the devious salesmen.

06 The survivor of the plane crash said that it had been a _____ and nightmarish experience.

07 I'm taking a _____ from watching movies and TV until my final exams are over.

08 The _____ would do anything for his powerful leader.

09 From upstairs, it sounded like her argumentative parents were finally in _____ once more.

10 I could tell he _____ from a different region of the country based on his Northern accent.

LESSON TWENTY-TWO

B. Fill in the blanks in the passage with the most appropriate words.
Passage 22:

Lucas is a _____ young student at Elm Tree High School. He is in four different clubs and has been in the student body government for two years in a row. He is taking a _____ as student body treasurer this year, however. This is because he is going to join the hiking club! Two of his friends, Mike and Dustin, are sad he won't be in the student government anymore. They acted as his campaign _____ in the last student election and loved cheering Lucas on during the debate events. Lucas's _____ was unmatched as far as debates went. Though his opponents often _____ from families of lawyers, professors, and doctors, Lucas is determined. His adolescent years had been somewhat _____; between the ages of two and six, he moved between countless foster homes and orphanages. Most of the orphanages were as warm and welcoming as a dark, mouldy _____; others were already teeming with adopted children whose needs couldn't be met. Growing up in the foster system had been a _____ experience. Therefore, Lucas was all too relieved to finally be adopted into a loving home with foster parents who supported Lucas's dreams. They were not _____, self-absorbed, or neglectful like many parents Lucas had heard about from the other orphaned kids. His foster parents were kind, and he felt _____ and a sense belonging in their house. It was because of his foster parents that Lucas had grown into such a bright and ambitious young student!

LESSON TWENTY-THREE

Target Words

1. Hibernal
2. Hierarchy
3. Histrionic
4. Idolatrous
5. Illusory
6. Immaculate
7. Immutable
8. Impecunious
9. Impervious
10. Impudent

A. Fill in the blanks with the most appropriate words.

01 There's a _____ chill in the air, and December is right around the corner.

02 His inability to respect the military's _____ got him kicked out.

03 Mary and Mason have an _____ love for one another, and we aren't sure it's healthy.

04 He can be very _____ if things don't go his way!

05 I took my car in for a wash. Afterwards, it was _____.

06 Kids from _____ homes are given free lunches and school supplies.

07 She relayed the story of her perilous camping trip in a _____ way that left us on the edge of our seats.

08 He is _____ when it comes to picking restaurants. He never wants to try new foods.

09 The tree house looks secure from the outside, but its reliability is _____. It will probably collapse as soon as someone goes inside it!

10 During dangerous situations, police wear gear that is _____ to bullets.

LESSON TWENTY-THREE

B. Fill in the blanks in the passage with the most appropriate words.
Passage 23:

It was a blustery _____ day in Vancouver, and despite the cold, Sara and her husband Kevin decided to go to the museum. The museum was located downtown in an _____ town square that was kept up by the city's cleaning crews. They stopped for coffee at an _____ little coffee shop that had, in its 70 years of business, never changed its menu or décor. People liked that even though the world changed around it, the café did not. It seemed _____ to trends and time itself! After getting coffee, they walked to the museum. First they went to the ancient art section. Many of the older pieces told stories about long-gone civilizations and _____ that had, for one reason or another, not withstood the tests of time. Next they went to the abstract art section. Sara liked abstract art because of its _____ quality; themes and messages were not so obvious to the average observer. You had to look closer. She felt an _____ love in particular for Jean-Michel Basquiat. Basquiat's art contrasted the lives of the wealthy elite with those from _____ backgrounds. They listened to a _____ museum guide explain how Basquiat had climbed the ranks to become one of the greatest artists of the past century. One _____ museum-goer loudly proclaimed that Basquiat's work "wasn't that great", but he was silenced when Kevin retorted, "I'd like to see you do better!" Sara stifled a giggle, and they headed into the next room to see more of the art.

LESSON TWENTY-FOUR

Target Words

1. Incessant
2. Incisive
3. Inclement
4. Inclination
5. Indictment
6. Indignation
7. Inextricable
8. Infuse
9. Ingenious
10. Inimical

A. Fill in the blanks with the most appropriate words.

01. The _____ honking of car horns during rush hour gave Moby a headache.

02. As far as the time traveller was concerned, the past, present, and future were _____.

03. The author's work is _____ with the pains of growing up poor.

04. The wolf gave an _____ growl that made the other, smaller wolf turn tail and run.

05. The letter demanding she leave the company left her with a sour feeling of _____.

06. My _____ to be brutally honest doesn't always serve me well in certain situations.

07. She stared at me with _____ eyes that made me feel vulnerable.

08. The _____ director was able to work with a miniscule budget and still produce an award-winning film.

09. The _____ seas made the people aboard the cruise ship anxious.

10. The news showed a segment about the _____ of four people involved in drug trafficking.

LESSON TWENTY-FOUR

B. Fill in the blanks in the passage with the most appropriate words.
Passage 24:

I don't usually like to leave my house on days when it's cold or stormy. _____ weather makes me feel sleepy, but Brooke insisted we go see the new horror movie. It was directed by an _____ filmmaker whose last film had won many awards. As we drove to the theatre, the rain was _____ and fell on the windshield of her car in big, wet drops. The clouds were dark and _____ in the sky, and it seemed as if the storm would soon worsen. I suggested we see the movie some other day when the weather wasn't so terrible. Brooke gave me an _____ look that told me there was no turning back. She had an _____ for seeing movies on rainy days, so it was obvious she wouldn't let me back out now; in her mind, films and bad weather were _____. In the end, I was glad she took me to the theatre. The movie was _____ with a sense of dread, and the end was very climactic. The main character of the movie died! At first, I felt _____ on behalf of the character because her death had seemed unfair. Afterwards, Brooke and I got hot chocolate and discussed the movie. She said that the character's death was necessary because otherwise they would have faced an _____ from the other characters. Ending the film with the character's death was the only way to resolve the chaos that character had caused.

LESSON TWENTY-FIVE

Target Words

1. Iniquity
2. Innate
3. Innocuous
4. Inquisitor
5. Inundate
6. Invariable
7. Invective
8. Inveterate
9. Irascible
10. Jubilant

A. Fill in the blanks with the most appropriate words.

01. Once I learned of Martin's _____, I divorced him. I would never forgive his infidelity.

02. Fortunately, the rent in our building is _____. Though the cost of living may rise, our rent will stay the same.

03. Christmas always puts me in a cheerful, _____ mood.

04. The wrestler seemed _____ at first glance, but once he got onto the mat, he turned into a beast!

05. His _____ and excessive drinking led his friends to wonder if he was an alcoholic.

06. Detective Rhodes felt more like an _____ than a detective at times, especially when a suspect had to be questioned for hours on end.

07. Shelley called me _____, and I only served to prove her point when I started yelling at her.

08. His _____ talent for learning languages led him to become a polyglot.

09. The journalist confronted the senator and unleashed _____ upon him.

10. "Flooding" is a psychological term in which the psychiatrist _____ his patient with whatever he fears most in hopes that the patient will overcome his fears through forced confrontation.

LESSON TWENTY-FIVE

B. Fill in the blanks in the passage with the most appropriate words.
Passage 25:

The _____ had been questioning his suspect for nearly six hours. The suspect, a man by the name of Frances, was facing questioning because of his recent _____: he had robbed a pie shop! Not only had he stolen all the money in their cash register, but he had also taken three cherry pies! When they learned the thief was in captivity, the pie shop owners came to the jail and hurled _____ at the man. They were normally a _____ elderly couple, but they were furious that someone had robbed them. They _____ him with insults and questions of their own. The detective, an _____ man at the best of times, soon became irritated by all the yelling, and asked the pie shop owners to leave. He knew the couple fairly well because he was an _____ pie purchaser. His tastes were _____ though, and he always bought blueberry pies. Once the pie shop owners were gone, the thief looked at him with seemingly _____ eyes and declared his innocence. However, the detective had an _____ talent for knowing when a person was lying, and could not be easily fooled!

LESSON TWENTY-SIX

Target Words

1. Judicious
2. Juvenile
3. Juxtapose
4. Labyrinthine
5. Laceration
6. Lachrymose
7. Latent
8. Laud
9. Laudatory
10. Lavish

A. Fill in the blanks with the most appropriate words.

01 They live in a _____ four-story mansion in Beverly Hills, California.

02 The _____ on his arm became infected, and he had to go to the hospital.

03 We walked through the _____ gardens and had to ask for directions more than once.

04 There was a fire in the office building, but the manager's _____ course of action prevented any injuries.

05 Her _____ refusal to give up her puppy made her parents rethink their cruel punishment.

06 I didn't discover my _____ talent for sculpting until I took an art class in college.

07 Dr. Becker _____ his patient for starting an exercise routine to combat obesity and heart failure.

08 Eric thought the new Star Wars movie was very _____ – as though it had been written for only young children and not adults too.

09 My publisher's _____ remarks about my new book put me in high spirits.

10 Basquiat's art _____ the life of the wealthy elite with that of people from impoverished backgrounds.

LESSON TWENTY-SIX

B. Fill in the blanks in the passage with the most appropriate words.
Passage 26:

Cassie and Vanessa went to a corn maze. They were worried it might be too _____, but when they got there, they were shocked. The corn maze was huge! Cassie _____ Vanessa for discovering the website for the corn maze, which had provided the address. There were _____ reviews on the website as well. Vanessa had made a _____ decision and decided it would be a perfect place to visit on a nice, autumn day. Next to the corn maze was an enormous, _____ pumpkin patch and a playground. The hyperactive, joyful children _____ with their tired, overworked parents made Cassie and Vanessa laugh. They passed a _____ young boy begging his parents to let him walk the corn maze by himself, but one of the employees of the maze warned the boy that it was more daunting than it looked. Cassie had a _____ sense of direction, so she wasn't worried about getting lost. They walked through the _____ corn field for two hours. At one point, Vanessa got snagged on a low-hanging stalk and suffered a small _____ to the arm, but luckily it didn't bleed. They were very tired once they finally reached the end of the maze!

LESSON TWENTY-SEVEN

Target Words

1. Lethargic
2. Lewd
3. Libel
4. Licentious
5. Limber
6. Limpid
7. Linchpin
8. Lithe
9. Loquacious
10. Lull

A. Fill in the blanks with the most appropriate words.

01 She is suing him for _____ because he called her a scam artist in his New York Times article.

02 The gymnast stretched and made sure she was _____ before the competition.

03 I feel very _____ today. It might be the rain making me so sleepy.

04 My aunts are very _____ at family get-togethers, especially if alcohol is involved!

05 The author's _____, straightforward prose made the book an easy, comprehendible read.

06 The song lyrics are quite _____, so naturally my parents disapprove.

07 People accuse her of being _____ and promiscuous, which hurts her feelings.

08 Brushing your teeth and flossing are the _____ of dental hygiene!

09 There was a _____ in the conversation. Grace used the opportunity to announce her recent promotion.

10 The _____ antelope jumped over the river with such ease and elegance that it seemed to fly.

LESSON TWENTY-SEVEN

B. Fill in the blanks in the passage with the most appropriate words.
Passage 27:

Though Devon had been a _____ of the fitness club since its inception five years ago, he was not immune from being fired. An online review for the club had surfaced, which claimed the reviewer had caught Devon spying on women in the locker rooms! Devon denied this _____ act and told his boss he wanted to sue the reviewer for _____. However, the boss was suspicious. He asked Jessica, the _____ yoga instructor, to hide out in the locker room and wait to see if Devon sneaked in. She was very _____ from practicing yoga daily, so she was able to squeeze into a perfect hiding spot. Meanwhile, Devon was in the break room telling anyone who would listen that he was innocent. The other employees were sick of his _____ claims of innocence, and they all thought he was guilty. They had listened to him for days now and were becoming _____ and tired of the whole issue. Finally, there was a _____ in the conversation, and the break room fell silent as Devon waited for validation. No one spoke up. As it grew closer to closing time, a few employees left work for the day. However, Jessica was still hiding in the locker room. Devon's _____ desire to spy on women in the locker room soon became _____ and undeniable to both his boss and Jessica. Jessica saw him walk into the locker room and hide in one of the showers! She was shocked and disgusted. She immediately went to the boss about her discovery, and Devon was fired on the spot.

LESSON TWENTY-EIGHT

Target Words

1. Luminescence
2. Magnanimous
3. Malaise
4. Malevolent
5. Malicious
6. Malign
7. Malleable
8. Mandatory
9. Manifest
10. Manifold

A. Fill in the blanks with the most appropriate words.

01 The antagonist's _____ nature is obscured by his charisma and small stature.

02 The implications of his comment were _____ and left journalists perplexed.

03 If you _____ someone publicly, be prepared to face the consequences.

04 The witch has not always been so _____. Once, she was a kind and generous princess.

05 The jewellery maker uses pliers to bend the _____ silver wire around the crystal charms.

06 The lake glowed with an ethereal _____ that could not be explained.

07 The teacher told her students that completing homework assignments was _____.

08 He _____ certain traits that make the psychiatrist wonder if he might be a psychopath.

09 After being stuck indoors for a week due to the snowstorm, I felt a strong sense of _____.

10 The philanthropist is a _____ member of society whose generosity seemingly knows no bounds.

LESSON TWENTY-EIGHT

B. Fill in the blanks in the passage with the most appropriate words.

Passage 28:

Anyone who knew Harold prior to December would have called him a _____ philanthropist. However, some facts came to light that would _____ Harold and ruin his career. Harold had been accused of harassment by a woman who used to be his secretary. Soon, _____ accusations about Harold began popping up. At first, Harold dismissed the accusations as nothing more than a _____, attention-seeking stunt. He claimed that the Me Too movement had made young women less _____ to the rules of a patriarchal society. In a _____ public speech, he exclaimed that women were lesser humans than men. He even claimed that it should be _____ for women to be paid less than men! People were horrified. A _____ grew within Harold's company and was _____ in a worker's revolt. Harold was put on trial for his harassment of female workers. The women in his company glowed with a triumphant _____ that brought strength to the victims of Harold's licentious wrongdoings.

LESSON TWENTY-NINE

Target Words

1. Masticate
2. Matrimony
3. Maudlin
4. Maxim
5. Meagre (US Meager)
6. Mediate
7. Melodramatic
8. Mendacious
9. Mercurial
10. Meritorious

A. Fill in the blanks with the most appropriate words.

01. The cows _____ grass slowly, their jaws moving in a slow circle.

02. I was paid a _____ hourly wage when I worked at the ice cream store.

03. The actress was let go from the production for being too _____.

04. She believed her book would be _____ and was shocked when it turned out to be a flop.

05. Evan looked forward to his future _____. He hoped to marry a wonderful person one day.

06. People with mood disorders can sometimes be _____ and unpredictable.

07. I refute the _____ that actions speak louder than words.

08. Will attempted to _____ a peace accord between the two countries.

09. The administration released _____ propaganda that would come back to bite them in the end.

10. I felt quite _____ after watching the nature documentary, so I signed up to volunteer at the animal shelter.

LESSON TWENTY-NINE

B. Fill in the blanks in the passage with the most appropriate words.
Passage 29:

A month before Audrey was supposed to be wed in holy _____ to her fiancé Cooper, she was admitted to an eating disorder clinic. Audrey was _____ when it came to food, to say the least. Some days she would gorge herself, and sometimes she would go days without eating. Her mother used to say Audrey was _____ and over-concerned when it came to her weight. This hurt Audrey's feelings immensely, and she had therefore learned to be _____ about her eating habits. Cooper had noticed that as the wedding grew closer, Audrey's meal portions became more and more _____. He finally decided to intervene and to _____ the issue between Audrey and her mother when he realized that all Audrey had eaten for the last two days was a single red apple. Audrey broke down in tears. With _____ honesty, she confessed her eating disorder. Cooper told her it was brave and _____ of her to confide in him, and he vowed to get her help. He took her to a clinic that specialized in eating disorders. There, Audrey learned many helpful _____ that she could repeat to herself in times of despair. Once she had said to herself every day, "Nothing tastes as good as skinny feels." However, now when she _____ and ate her meals, she told herself, "Love yourself first, and everything else falls into line."

LESSON THIRTY

Target Words

1. Metamorphosis
2. Mimic
3. Misogyny
4. Modicum
5. Mollify
6. Monogamy
7. Mores
8. Morose
9. Munificent
10. Mutability

A. Fill in the blanks with the most appropriate words.

01 He prides himself on his _____. In just two years, he has lived in four different cities!

02 After his fish died, Jacob felt very _____.

03 _____ is the standard for most, but some people practice polyamory.

04 She is lucky to have _____ parents who will financially support her until she has a job.

05 This bird can _____ human speech. You can train it to say things!

06 Her _____ are questionable. Last week I saw her steal candy at a gas station.

07 He underwent a spiritual _____ after attending a five-day meditation retreat.

08 Telling her to "calm down" during a fight will do the opposite of _____ her.

09 The witness made a statement that did not contain a _____ of truth.

10 Unfortunately, the president of our country is guilty of _____. He objectifies even his own wife!

LESSON THIRTY

B. Fill in the blanks in the passage with the most appropriate words.
Passage 30:

Clara quit her job due to the daily _____ she faced at the hands of her narcissistic boss. She was sick of his grabby hands and offensive jokes, so she moved with her boyfriend Peter to Maine. During the first few weeks in Maine, Clara was _____ and downtrodden. She was worried she didn't have the _____ that Peter had. In their seven years of _____, she had seen him jump from job to job with relative ease. She wanted to _____ his adaptability, so she kicked her job hunt into overdrive. She was losing her last _____ of hope when she finally got a callback from a bookstore. Clara went in for an interview but was shocked to find the man who ran the bookstore was another misogynist! His _____ concerning women were just as appalling as her old boss. Clara had hoped moving to Maine would jumpstart a _____ in her career but was now wondering if she had been too hopeful. Her _____ husband listened patiently as Clara vented about how terribly the interview had gone. He tried to _____ her with a glass of wine, which definitely helped. Clara was thankful to have him, and he promised to help her find a job that week.

LESSON THIRTY-ONE

Target Words

1. Myopic
2. Myriad
3. Narrate
4. Nebulous
5. Nefarious
6. Neologism
7. Neonate
8. Noisome
9. Notoriety
10. Novel

A. Fill in the blanks with the most appropriate words.

01 It's difficult to explain to the hotheaded Henry the _____ concept of meditation.

02 Audiobooks are a great way to consume literature. You can listen to someone _____ a story while you do things like drive to work, fold laundry, or make dinner!

03 Barry hadn't showered in three weeks. As a result, he was extremely _____.

04 Robert and Margot Charleston have three children: two twin girls and a little _____ boy.

05 Something about her grin seemed _____. I wondered what terrible things she was up to.

06 It was a bit _____ of me to assume you couldn't win the competition.

07 The young scientist has _____ ideas about how to solve global warming.

08 Netflix contains _____ movies, TV shows, and documentaries to choose from.

09 Jack Kerouac is a practitioner of _____. He invented the term "beatnik."

10 President Nixon gained historical _____ for his involvement in the Watergate scandal.

LESSON THIRTY-ONE

B. Fill in the blanks in the passage with the most appropriate words.
Passage 31:

Oliver had written and published four books. Each of his books had been more _____ than the last, and his fans praised him for his originality and creativity. Some considered him a master of _____, for his books contained silly, made up terms like "bogbin" and "hellcrux," which had become standard vocabulary for his adoring readers! Each of his four books covered _____ topics. His first had been about a man who came into _____ for murdering his sister and her _____ child. His second book had explored the _____ concept of extraterrestrial life in the galaxy and followed a young pilot on her explorations through space.

Oliver was having trouble writing his fifth book, though. This was in part due to his neighbour, Gabe. Sometimes Oliver wondered if Gabe really was the ailing, old man he presented to the world, or if in fact he was actually some _____ super-villain sent from the underworld to stop Oliver from writing a fifth book! You see, Gabe had a garden, and this garden was right on the edge of his land. Oliver could smell the garden from his backyard patio, which is where he did most of his writing. Unfortunately, Gabe's garden was extremely _____. Whatever he was growing smelled like rotting fish! Though Oliver was _____ and had to wear glasses, he could plainly see the culprit: a Bradford Pear tree. So, one day, Oliver went over to Gabe's garden while Gabe wasn't home, and he did the unthinkable: he cut down the tree! Though he had to pay a fine and apologize to Gabe, he had a new story to _____ to his readers: the story of Oliver versus the foul-smelling Bradford Pear tree

LESSON THIRTY-TWO

Target Words

1. Noxious
2. Obdurate
3. Obfuscate
4. Obsequious
5. Odious
6. Officious
7. Olfactory
8. Ominous
9. Oration
10. Ostracize

A. Fill in the blanks with the most appropriate words.

01 The hunter was _____ from his tribe for hunting and killing the sacred white buffalo.

02 Adolf Hitler was an _____ German dictator responsible for millions of deaths.

03 Though the writer can pen best-selling novels, his public _____ could use a bit of work.

04 She _____ the results of the competition by spilling black paint on the winning ballot.

05 Hilda finds her sister's _____ nature a bit annoying. She wishes her sister would act rebellious for a change!

06 The debate was full of _____ comments and ad hominem insults rather than civilized discourse.

07 He has firm, _____ opinions concerning the sanctity of marriage and monogamy.

08 The _____ bystander tried to make himself useful, but he only complicated things.

09 If I had to choose between my _____ senses and sight, I would definitely pick sight.

10 I asked my boss if I was being fired, but there followed only a heavy, _____ silence.

LESSON THIRTY-TWO

B. Fill in the blanks in the passage with the most appropriate words.
Passage 32:

Since he was a teenager, Kent had always loved to be active in the community. Though some might call him _____, Kent just wanted to be useful. There were far too many _____ things in the world, like poverty, starvation, depression, and crime. He aspired to be a compassionate member of society, however _____ it made him seem to community leaders he admired. Nevertheless, something changed when Kent got into a car accident. It had been a rainy day; looking back, Kent realized how _____ the dark weather had been. He wished he had just stayed home! The heavy rainfall had obscured the lines on the road, making it difficult to discern where one lane ended and the other began. He also had a terrible cold. His _____ senses were shot, he sneezed every couple of minutes, and his eyes were swollen and glassy. Within an instant, he had suddenly lost control of the car. To this day, he is _____ about the belief that an angel was watching over him and will not allow any rationalizations to _____ that belief. His car swerved to one side of the road, and he crashed into a telephone pole. _____ fumes came from under the crumpled hood of his car, and his airbags had gone off. Still, Kent considered himself lucky. On the other side of the road there was only a cliff. Though his social skills and _____ have suffered since the accident, the community has paid back the empathy and kindness that Kent contributed all through the years! He has had a visitor in the hospital every day since the accident!

LESSON THIRTY-THREE

Target Words

1. Pacify
2. Paragon
3. Pariah
4. Parody
5. Patent
6. Pedagogue
7. Pellucid
8. Penchant
9. Peregrinate
10. Perfunctory

A. Fill in the blanks with the most appropriate words.

01 The border agent gave him a _____ glance before admitting him into the country.

02 Her _____ for wearing gold makes her look ostentatious in most crowds.

03 Galileo went from scientist to _____ after he publicly claimed the Earth was not the centre of the universe.

04 As far as medical students go, the hardworking, whip-smart and steadfast Lucia is a _____.

05 Your _____ and desperate desire to date Annalise makes me a little queasy.

06 At Saint Cecilia's Catholic private school, the _____ are all nuns or priests.

07 The sun shone down on the _____, tranquil waters of Hemlock Lake.

08 Her nature to _____ has made her a lifelong runner and evening walker.

09 The opening band couldn't _____ the crowd's impatience, so they left the stage early.

10 The 2012 movie *Cabin in the Woods* is a _____ of most horror movies.

LESSON THIRTY-THREE

B. Fill in the blanks in the passage with the most appropriate words.
Passage 33:

Christine had a _____ for both learning and teaching. She had been a tutor in high school and knew since she was 15 that she wanted to pursue a career as a _____. Many of her classmates wanted to be scientists, athletes, or doctors; they thought her desire to teach was a _____ decision, as if she had had no choice in the matter! Christine felt like a _____ sometimes. People questioned her teaching aspirations, but she refused to _____ them by turning away from her vocation! The first year in her teaching program would be a _____ experiment to see if she was cut out to be a teacher. It took intelligence, patience, empathy, and hard work to run a classroom! Soon she rose to the top of her class; Christine was a _____! She had one, _____ goal for over a decade: become a teacher. Her goal was finally within reach! A few years later, after Christine graduated, she spent two months _____ across the US, visiting different cities. Eventually, Christine decided to live and work in Seattle. It would be a _____ of the truth to say that Christine hadn't made her dreams come true, for indeed she had.

LESSON THIRTY-FOUR

Target Words

1. Permeate
2. Persevere
3. Pertinacious
4. Peruse
5. Pervasive
6. Petulance
7. Physiognomy
8. Pique
9. Pithy
10. Pittance

A. Fill in the blanks with the most appropriate words.

01. Olga has only a _____ of sympathy for homeless people.

02. I am sick of his _____ in the workplace, so I am reporting him to the manager!

03. Coffee and yoga help me _____ through final exams.

04. Her _____ remark about the state of our country left me to bask in silent contemplation.

05. He _____ the encyclopedia, carefully reading subjects regarding the history of archaeology.

06. My mom can be very _____. When she thinks she's right, nothing will change her mind.

07. An anxious feeling _____ the crowd, and soon a riot started.

08. When I learned my doctor practiced _____, I quit going to him.

09. My careless sister _____ me when she told me I looked like I had gained weight.

10. Public speaking is a _____ and common fear for many people in this country.

LESSON THIRTY-FOUR

B. Fill in the blanks in the passage with the most appropriate words.
Passage 34:

Lucille is in grad school, and her thesis focuses on _____ racism in the northeastern parts of the United States. One particular field of study that she found to be rooted in prejudice and racism was _____, the study of facial features. Lucille spoke to many different doctors about this so-called science. She was especially _____ by one doctor's claim that it was a legitimate science when he had no evidence to support his claim. He was quite _____ about his stance. He even asked if he could examine the shape of her head and her facial features to determine her personality traits! She thought his request revealed his own _____ and naivety.

Lucille also interviewed teachers who work in inner-city schools. She had a brief but _____ conversation with one teacher who remarked how his inner-city school had fewer resources than wealthy public or private schools. To him, the meagre _____ of school resources spoke volumes about a societal lack of empathy for less fortunate school children. Lucille was determined to publicize the systemic racism that _____ American culture. Lucille has _____ many studies on racism in America, and though she feels downtrodden about it at times, she knows she must _____. She hopes her thesis will take steps towards addressing and ending racism in America.

LESSON THIRTY-FIVE

Target Words

1. Placate
2. Placid
3. Plethora
4. Pliable
5. Poach
6. Poised
7. Polygamy
8. Portentous
9. Portly
10. Precarious

A. Fill in the blanks with the most appropriate words.

01. Roger felt self-conscious about his _____ physique, so he signed up for a gym membership.

02. Wildlife conservationists are vocal about the heartbreaking consequences of _____.

03. The bridge swayed in the wind, hundreds of feet above land. Its _____ appearance terrified me.

04. She owns a _____ of true crime books that you can borrow anytime.

05. Many people prefer monogamy to _____, which some find licentious and indecent.

06. The cat stood _____ on the roof, scanning the courtyard below for unsuspecting mice.

07. The woodworker uses Western Red Cedar, which is an extremely _____ type of wood.

08. Christmastime is Alice's favourite time of year because it is so cheerful and _____.

09. The _____ weather forecast was predicting a devastating category-5 hurricane.

10. The riot police were there to _____ the crowd, but their presence only made matters worse.

LESSON THIRTY-FIVE

B. Fill in the blanks in the passage with the most appropriate words.

Passage 35:

After a _____ skiing expedition in the Swiss Alps, Becket decided he had had his fill of adventure for the time being. He had come dangerously close to losing his life on one particularly _____ day of the trip. Though he had a _____ of safety knowledge and wilderness training, nothing could have prepared him for the experience of falling down a tree well. Tree wells are caused by loose snow building up around the trunk of a tree, and you can actually suffocate if you fall down one! Becket and his friend James had gone skiing one morning. James was in the middle of discussing the merits of _____ versus traditional marriage when Becket suddenly lost control of his skis and went barreling into a tree. He was not a _____ person, so his slender figure had fallen headfirst deep into the tree well. James hurried over to help. He tried to _____ Becket, who was terrified. James told him to be _____ and to stop moving around too much. If he kept moving, snow would fall into the tree well, and Becket might suffocate! Becket tried to stay _____ in his dangerous position while James called for help. While he waited, Becket had a lot of time to think about his life. He wondered if this was how endangered animals felt when they were _____: trapped, on the verge of death, and absolutely terrified for their lives. When help finally arrived, the rescuers used a _____ type of cord to tie to Becket's feet, and then they used a snowmobile to pull him out. Becket was so relieved to have been saved. He vowed from that day forward to be more careful when skiing!

LESSON THIRTY-SIX

Target Words

1. Predestination
2. Premonition
3. Preponderance
4. Presage
5. Prestidigitation
6. Presumptuous
7. Profane
8. Profuse
9. Propensity
10. Propriety

A. Fill in the blanks with the most appropriate words.

01. It was _____ that made us meet and fall in love!

02. The tornado sirens blaring across the county were a _____ of the oncoming storm.

03. Yasmina prides herself on her _____ and good manners.

04. Tyrese plays rugby and football. He has a _____ for contact sports!

05. He is so talented with _____ that he could be a con artist or pickpocket!

06. Oliver told the new female student he would be her boyfriend if she wanted one, but she thought it was an extremely _____ offer.

07. I had a _____ that I would get into a car accident, so I decided to stay home that day.

08. The beekeeper was confused about the _____ of wasps attracted to his hive.

09. The _____ and extravagant decorations for the Christmas gala had everyone talking.

10. He was excommunicated from the Church for being _____.

LESSON THIRTY-SIX

B. Fill in the blanks in the passage with the most appropriate words.
Passage 36:

Morgana had always known she was a little bit psychic. From a young age, she had believed in _____ and frequently told her classmates their destiny in exchange for a candy bar or new pen. Her _____ for fortune telling had shown itself early. When she was just seven years old, she begged her mom and dad not to leave for a vacation trip to Jamaica. Their car breaking down on the way to the airport was a _____ of what happened next: the plane that they would have gotten on had ended up crashing, and most of the passengers had died! Morgana's parents at first thought her gift was _____; they were religious people and worried her powers were sacrilegious. However, when the pastor learned of Morgana's gifts, he told them to practice _____ and patience in regard to her talent. As long as she wasn't developing her gift for _____ or magical trickery, it could be useful! Later in life, Morgana recognized that a _____ of people could benefit from her clairvoyance. She worried that starting a business of fortune telling might be considered _____ among the people in her community, but they flocked to her door like bees to a flower! She offered her _____ talents to whoever came to her door. People were fascinated by her _____ of the future!

LESSON THIRTY-SEVEN

Target Words

1. Protean
2. Prudent
3. Puerile
4. Pugnacious
5. Pulchritude
6. Punctilious
7. Pungent
8. Purport
9. Putrid
10. Quaint

A. Fill in the blanks with the most appropriate words.

01. Sometimes political news can be difficult to keep up with. It has an elusive, _____ quality.

02. She _____ not to have been there at the time of the accident, but video footage proves otherwise.

03. When he got home from his two-week trip, he realized he had forgotten to take out the trash before he had left. His house was _____!

04. We were very _____ in planning a Thanksgiving dinner party this year.

05. I hear my _____ upstairs neighbours arguing and stomping around almost every night!

06. Kate's _____ jokes don't help her get many dates.

07. Montmartre is a _____ part of Paris where artists linger and streets wind down little hills.

08. If she had been more _____ while driving, she could have avoided the car accident.

09. I am stunned by the _____ of Van Gogh's paintings. They are so exquisite!

10. Something _____ is coming from the refrigerator.

LESSON THIRTY-SEVEN

B. Fill in the blanks in the passage with the most appropriate words.
Passage 37:

Mark and Ella decided to have a _____ Thanksgiving get-together, so they invited all of their friends and family. Thanksgiving is a _____ holiday that manifests itself in many different ways and traditions. Ella's family would be running a charity marathon on Thanksgiving morning. They were a _____ bunch, and they had their traditions. However, Ella wondered about their intentions behind running the race. Did they really care about the cause behind the marathon, or were they just _____ about fitness and staying healthy? Mark, Ella's husband, had long ago smoked cigarettes. When Ella had mentioned this to her family, they commented that his smoking habit was _____. They thought smoking was disgusting, and that the _____ smell of cigarette smoke was _____. On that, Ella could agree with them. When Ella first suggested to Mark that he quit smoking, he became _____ and defensive. Ella tried to reason with him, and eventually he listened. Deep down he knew there was no _____ or glory about being addicted to cigarettes. Quitting smoking was very hard for him. Once Ella had asked how many cigarettes he had smoked over the past week, and he _____ to have smoked a number very different from the truth. That was the only time he had ever lied, though, and within three months, he had quit smoking completely!

LESSON THIRTY-EIGHT

Target Words

1. Quid pro quo
2. Quotidian
3. Radiant
4. Rancid
5. Ratiocinate
6. Raze
7. Recalcitrant
8. Recalibrate
9. Recapitulate
10. Rectify

A. Fill in the blanks with the most appropriate words.

01 After being released from prison, Oliver set out to _____ his past crimes.

02 The film club gets together for a movie night every Tuesday. Afterwards, they _____ and discuss the film over dinner.

03 I accidentally left fruit on the counter while I was away, so it was _____ by the time I returned.

04 She flashes me a _____ smile and cheerfully waves goodbye before getting onto her plane.

05 A construction company is _____ the old apartment complex next door to build a preschool.

06 I suggested a _____: he could borrow my car if he let me use his video game console.

07 Why didn't our _____ delivery of the local newspaper arrive today?

08 The witness gave a _____ response when asked a serious question by the defense team's lawyer.

09 I don't want to _____ old arguments, but you haven't changed a bit!

10 The computer was _____ after the programmer made a few adjustments to the system.

LESSON THIRTY-EIGHT

B. Fill in the blanks in the passage with the most appropriate words.
Passage 38:

Oliver never imagined he would go to prison one day. He had been a well-behaved boy in his youth. He tackled every _____ chore with aplomb and never misbehaved. People who knew him best would never describe Oliver as _____ because he was so disciplined and obedient. However, after Oliver met Cade, all of that changed. Cade was a charismatic young delinquent, and he had a way of sweet-talking people into doing favours for him. On one such occasion, Cade offered Oliver a _____ agreement: if Oliver helped Cade hack a security system, he would pay Oliver $50,000. Oliver needed the money, so he agreed. Being a computer genius, Oliver knew he could _____ any security system with ease. But soon it became clear that the security system he was hacking belonged to a bank! While Oliver was _____ the security systems, Cade had hired a team of men to rob the headquarters. And thus, Oliver had landed himself in prison. Cade's deal had, metaphorically, been _____ when first proposed to Oliver, but Oliver had chosen to ignore the warning signs. He had plenty of time to _____ over the crime while in prison, yet he remained positive. He would _____ himself once he got out, atoning for his crimes through community service. With zero intent on _____ his criminal ways, he knew he could make a future for himself. Oliver hoped it would be a _____ one.

LESSON THIRTY-NINE

Target Words

1. Redact
2. Redoubtable
3. Redress
4. Reel
5. Refrain
6. Reiterate
7. Relish
8. Remiss
9. Render
10. Renovate

A. Fill in the blanks with the most appropriate words.

01. Judge Peter is a _____ older gentleman who has a forbidding presence.

02. She wanted to _____ her financial problems, so she came up with a budget plan.

03. Helene _____ the taste of elderflower wine.

04. It would be _____ to go to class without a pen and paper!

05. Todd ran his bike into the telephone pole, which sent him _____.

06. The end of the film _____ me speechless.

07. As an editor, Clara chose which parts of an article needed to be _____ before publication.

08. Sara and Kevin are _____ their kitchen to give it a more modern feel.

09. He couldn't _____ from asking her out on a date. He was in love!

10. My hearing isn't great, so I constantly have to ask people to _____ certain things.

LESSON THIRTY-NINE

B. Fill in the blanks in the passage with the most appropriate words.
Passage 39:

Senator O'Malley was scheduled for a live TV interview with Chris Coleman. As a _____ politician in his forties with liberal leanings and a strong sense of community, O'Malley was well-liked within his community. He _____ the opportunity to meet new people and to learn how to improve his city. Primarily, he hoped he could _____ the economic issues that many citizens faced. When he arrived at the TV station, he was informed that _____ were being done on the old studio to get the technology and set dressings up-to-date. Therefore, the interview would be held in Mr. Coleman's office. The office was on the top floor with a spectacular view of the city. Senator O'Malley was _____ silent--awestruck by the view. He wanted to _____ from mentioning his fear of heights, but Mr. Coleman noticed O'Malley's reluctance to go near the windows. In an attempt to counteract the senator's phobia, Mr. Coleman told O'Malley that being on the top floor used to make him _____. Senator O'Malley appreciated the gesture. Soon the men sat down, and the interview began. The senator was planning to run in the presidential race, so Chris Coleman asked a series of questions about O'Malley's more questionable past statements. Senator O'Malley did not try to _____ any of them. He knew it would be _____ to try to deny his past mistakes. He admitted that he had been wrong about things, but that he had ultimately grown from the experience and did not regret his words. He _____ his respect and love for the city and hoped its citizens would find him worthy of their vote in future elections.

LESSON FORTY

Target Words

1. Repose
2. Reprehensible
3. Repudiate
4. Repulse
5. Requisition
6. Restitution
7. Retaliation
8. Retract
9. Retribution
10. Revel (in)

A. Fill in the blanks with the most appropriate words.

01. After being hit by a car, Kathleen sought _____ from the driver to cover her hospital bills.

02. The CEO _____ a meeting to speak with his closest members on the board.

03. Billy shoved Parker at recess. In _____, Parker tripped Billy in the hallway.

04. I feel like I haven't had a moment of _____ in weeks. I'm exhausted!

05. That was a _____ thing you did, and I hope you get punished!

06. We do not _____ in the sound of barking dogs. Unfortunately, our neighbour has four.

07. The teacher _____ Connor's plea for an extra credit assignment.

08. I'm _____ my bet on the game because I don't want to lose money.

09. If someone ever hurt his family, Duke would unquestionably seek _____.

10. Stella hates the taste of ranch dressing. It _____ her!

LESSON FORTY

B. Fill in the blanks in the passage with the most appropriate words.
Passage 40:

Jason and Michael had been in an ongoing prank war for years. It started when they were kids. Jason had put a whoopee cushion on Michael's seat during class. In _____, Michael put peanut butter in Jason's shoes. They came up with rules to make sure their pranks never became malicious or _____. They did not _____ in seeing each other suffer. Instead, the prank war was about laughing. Humourless people repulsed them. Life, in their opinion, wasn't supposed to be taken seriously. As they got older, their _____ for past pranks grew more extreme. Once, while Michael was enjoying a moment of quiet _____, Jason had sneaked up behind him and dumped an enormous bucket of ice water on his head! Michael was furious. He demanded _____ for the suede armchair, which was ruined by the water. Jason apologized. He wished he could _____ his last prank and wondered if it had been too mean. Michael _____ a temporary cease-fire on their prank war. However, the truth was that his reaction to the ice water prank was an elaborate set-up! The armchair wasn't even suede, not that he would care about it anyway! It had _____ him to act so angry about an innocent prank. He _____ solemnity and sanctimoniousness. Jason would be so shocked when he found his car filled with rubber snakes in the morning…

LESSON FORTY-ONE

Target Words

1. Rife
2. Ruddy
3. Ruse
4. Rustic
5. Saccharine
6. Sacrosanct
7. Sagacious
8. Salient
9. Salutation
10. Sanguine

A. Fill in the blanks with the most appropriate words.

01 His comments were _____ with insinuations that I should lose some weight.

02 Politicians have to be extremely _____ when speaking out in public.

03 The man tilted his hat as a _____, and then formally introduced himself.

04 The soil here is _____, which tells you it is very fertile and perfect for planting crops!

05 The most _____ part of tonight's gala is the awards ceremony.

06 My _____ attitude is contagious. Soon, everyone else will be in a cheerful mood!

07 I thought she was actually sick with the measles, but she had fooled me. It was just a _____!

08 To me, her _____ way of treating people seemed insincere.

09 Marriage is a _____ union of two people who want to spend their lives together.

10 My mom loves _____ décor. She finds it charming and bucolic.

LESSON FORTY-ONE

B. Fill in the blanks in the passage with the most appropriate words.
Passage 41:

The sky was blue, and the day was _____ with sunshine. A warm breeze billowed across the river just as Skip drove up in his car. He noticed his friend Bobby was already there. Skip waved his hand to Bobby in _____. Bobby returned Skip's gesture with a bright, _____ smile, and then the two friends met by the water. Bobby had hauled his boat along with him, which he treated with so much affection, it was like it was _____. Though quite _____ and far from being sleek or modern, it was a great boat. When Skip had first seen that thing of Bobby's, he thought it was a _____; after all, how could Bobby love such a worn-out vessel? But Bobby's adoration was sincere!

Today the river was a _____ colour; a heavy storm had forced soil and sediment into the water, turning it a muddy reddish colour. Skip had brought his fishing gear with him. He was a _____ fisherman who always caught and released the fish back into the water. It was Skip's _____ opinion that killing and eating the fish wasn't the point of fishing. Rather, fishing with his friend Bobby was a time for them to reconnect and discuss their lives. Though Bobby's ceaseless cheerfulness could be _____ at times, Skip and Bobby had been friends for over three decades, and Bobby was a great friend. The two got into the boat, pushed it off into the water, and enjoyed their afternoon in the sun.

LESSON FORTY-TWO

Target Words

1. Sate
2. Satiate
3. Savour (US Savor)
4. Scathing
5. Scourge
6. Scurrilous
7. Sedate
8. Sedentary
9. Seer
10. Seminal

A. Fill in the blanks with the most appropriate words.

01 We were ravenous after our long hike and _____ our hunger the minute we got home.

02 Marie Curie made _____ discoveries that changed chemistry research forever.

03 Tom thinks the _____ is a scam artist. He doesn't believe in clairvoyance.

04 Edna was embarrassed by her sons' _____ behaviour at the dinner party.

05 His third-degree burns were extremely painful, so the medical staff _____ him.

06 The Bubonic Plague was a _____ in the Middle Ages that killed millions of people.

07 Laurie and Bart's wedding cake was so delicious; I _____ every bite!

08 Sloths are very _____ creatures; their name comes from the same word as "slow"!

09 Ella will _____ her desire to learn more by attending graduate school.

10 The reporter launched a _____ verbal attack on the president in the middle of the event!

LESSON FORTY-TWO

B. Fill in the blanks in the passage with the most appropriate words.
Passage 42:

No one would have ever described Richie as a kind person. He was a _____ man and seemed to pride himself on his ability to upset people. He frequently made _____ comments about people in his workplace, to the point that his boss actually fired him! Something inside Richie burned with a fiery fury. He had always been an angry person. No amount of medicine, exercise, or meditation could _____ his innate rage. As a child, he had been very overweight, which led to him being teased. He _____ his depression about being teased with food and lived a very _____ life for many years. However, he soon turned to bullying as a means of catharsis. Rather than relish the taste of various junk foods, he _____ the tears and shocked faces he could trigger in other people with just a few harsh words. Once Richie was fired from his job for being too cruel, he realized he needed to make some _____ life changes. His sister, Veronica, suggested Richie go to a _____ and have his fortune told, but Richie didn't believe in the supernatural. Still, he was curious, so he allowed Veronica to take him to the clairvoyant. Immediately the fortune-teller could sense the unbridled wrath that simmered inside of him. She told him his rage was like a _____ on his system. If he did not take the proper measures, it would consume him completely! The fortune-teller urged Richie to find ways to _____ and ultimately dissipate his anger, so Richie signed up for anger management in an attempt to turn his life around.

LESSON FORTY-THREE

Target Words

1. Serendipity
2. Slander
3. Sobriety
4. Somnolent
5. Sordid
6. Soothsayer
7. Spectral
8. Spurious
9. Stagnant
10. Stagnate

A. Fill in the blanks with the most appropriate words.

01. The solemn air of _____ in the funeral home was suffocating.

02. Construction of the building _____ after the inspector found numerous safety code violations.

03. Early in the morning, the lake looks completely _____ and devoid of all life.

04. The film paints a _____ picture of life in an Italian crime family.

05. Years ago, a _____ told me I would have four children. She was right!

06. The journalist apologized for _____ the actor, but the damage had already been done.

07. I was surprised to hear the author's "nonfiction" book was _____ and full of lies.

08. On her way to work, Meg found a fifty-dollar bill. It was a moment of pure _____!

09. Her pale skin and diaphanous dress give her a _____ appearance.

10. The overworked nurse constantly feels _____, no matter how much caffeine she drinks.

LESSON FORTY-THREE

B. Fill in the blanks in the passage with the most appropriate words.
Passage 43:

Olivia and Hugh had no idea their house was haunted when they first moved in. Years ago, Olivia had spoken to a _____ who told her that she would one day encounter a ghost. She had forgotten all about that forewarning. Olivia and Hugh thought it was _____ that led them to their new house. Within the first month, however, strange things began to happen. First, Olivia always felt _____, no matter how much sleep or coffee she had had. Second, Hugh was struggling with his _____. That _____ craving for alcohol, which had been _____ for years, was something he suddenly had trouble ignoring again. Both he and his wife Olivia knew something was wrong with the house, so they contacted the realtor who had sold it to them.

The realtor refused to meet them at the house after dark, so they asked her to come over the following morning. When the realtor arrived, her steps _____ as she approached the house. She glanced into a second floor window and nearly had a heart attack. There in the window, just barely visible, was a _____ figure staring down at her… and it wasn't Hugh or Olivia! The realtor called the couple on her cell phone and made a _____ attempt to explain why she couldn't come inside, but Hugh and Olivia saw through her lies. They met her outside in the front yard and proceeded to hound her about the history of the house. Eventually the realtor acquiesced and divulged the building's dark history. Olivia and Hugh were shocked. They swore to _____ the realtor for selling them haunted property, but the realtor just shrugged and wished them luck.

LESSON FORTY-FOUR

Target Words

1. Static
2. Steadfast
3. Strenuous
4. Strife
5. Stupefy
6. Submissive
7. Subsist
8. Succinct
9. Suffice
10. Supplant

A. Fill in the blanks with the most appropriate words.

01. Having been shipwrecked on a deserted island for three months, the survivors amazingly _____ on coconuts and wild game until their rescue.

02. Hiring a moving company is great for transporting heavy furniture. They can help you with the most _____ tasks!

03. Eleanor's disingenuous apology would not _____. She would have to try again and be more sincere.

04. The rate of unemployment has remained _____ despite the decreasing population.

05. I made sure vegetarian dishes _____ carnivorous ones this year in an attempt to be more environmentally conscious and animal-friendly.

06. Your _____ prejudices concerning people of a different race make me furious!

07. She _____ me with her charm, intellect, and contagious laughter.

08. The effect of a patriarchal society is that women are, from a young age, taught to be _____ towards men.

09. Please do not compare your _____ to mine. Both are valid.

10. My _____ and acerbic retort left them speechless.

LESSON FORTY-FOUR

B. Fill in the blanks in the passage with the most appropriate words.
Passage 44:

It was all over the news: a man named Jordan had been found in an underground tunnel after being trapped there for seven months. Jordan claimed he had _____ all that time on bugs, and on water that dripped from the pipes. People were _____ by his story. They hailed him for being so _____ in his determination to survive until he was found. Jordan was interviewed on dozens of television shows. The hosts expressed condolences that Jordan had experienced such harrowing _____. Jordan explained that he had had just enough water and protein to _____. He also usually cited his _____ sense of hope that eventually someone would find him. However, whenever asked how he had gotten stuck in the tunnel in the first place, Jordan always gave the same _____, enigmatic response: "The doors were locked."

A building manager who owned the premises came forward and explained that even if the doors were locked, it wouldn't require much _____ effort to kick them down. When a TV crew visited the tunnel for a news segment, they found a massive padlock on the door to the tunnel. The building manager claimed a new lock had _____ the old one after Jordan was discovered, but Jordan swore it was there all along. The building manager pressed charges against Jordan for bringing so much negative attention to him and his building. A detective brought Jordan in to question him about his seven-month survival fiasco, and it wasn't long until Jordan became _____ and admitted the entire story was made-up! He had simply wanted attention, and to be on TV.

LESSON FORTY-FIVE

Target Words

1. Surfeit
2. Surmise
3. Surreptitious
4. Swarthy
5. Sybarite
6. Sycophant
7. Sympathetic
8. Sympathy
9. Synopsis
10. Taciturn

A. Fill in the blanks with the most appropriate words.

01 After being questioned for ten hours straight, the suspect grew irritable and _____.

02 I found a plot _____ for the film on Wikipedia.

03 Nick seems comparatively pale next to his tanned, _____ sister.

04 Eleanor offered her deepest _____ to her friend, whose cat had just passed away.

05 I wish people were more _____ towards animals. The horror animals in slaughterhouses go through every day is nightmarish and cruel.

06 The hoarder's _____ of personal belongings has been out of control for years.

07 The movie star has been called a glutton, a hedonist, and a _____. She claims she simply has expensive tastes.

08 I couldn't listen to another superficial compliment this _____ had to say.

09 The assassin conducts his business in the most _____ way possible.

10 He _____ that he'd said the wrong thing when his wife started crying.

LESSON FORTY-FIVE

B. Fill in the blanks in the passage with the most appropriate words.
Passage 45:

The Russo family conducted their illicit meetings in the most _____ places they could find. The police and other crime families were always hot on their tail, so Ricky, the only son of Don Russo, had to be careful in finding meeting places. His _____, surly father rarely gave him advice on where they could meet because, in truth, Don Russo had become a bit of a _____. He no longer prided himself on his ability to network with important people and run an illegal business like a well-oiled machine; instead, he doted over his priceless artwork, his opulent four-story mansion, and his _____ of Ferraris, Lamborghinis, and Aston Martins. Even so, Ricky was _____ toward his father's voluptuary tastes. Don Russo had been born into a dirt-poor family and had climbed his way to the top over decades of painstaking work. But Ricky could only have _____ up to a point. His father's expensive distractions were taking a toll on the Russo family business. Ricky _____ it would soon be time for the Don to step down. Still, Ricky felt intimidated when his father's _____, cunning eyes landed on him each meeting. Ricky would begin each meeting with a _____ of the week's happenings. As he spoke, he would watch for any glint in the Don's eyes that he had disappointed him in some way. For ultimately, Ricky just wanted to support his father and be the best son he could be. He worried most of all that his father would think of him as a blubbering _____ of a son, riding on his father's coattails and waiting for him to finally die. In truth, however, Don Russo loved his son. He simply never learned how to say it.

LESSON FORTY-SIX

Target Words

1. Tantamount
2. Tedious
3. Telepathic
4. Tenuous
5. Terrestrial
6. Terse
7. Timorous
8. Tome
9. Toothsome
10. Torpid

A. Fill in the blanks with the most appropriate words.

01 His long-winded explanation of the history of the US Postal Service was honestly quite _____.

02 Billy's _____ response to her prolonged confession of love left Shelley blindsided and hurt.

03 Elena claims to be _____, but I've never seen her clairvoyance in action.

04 Global warming is having a devastating impact on all _____ and aquatic life.

05 The sloth is one of nature's most _____ creatures.

06 Melanie brought _____ hors d'oeuvres to the Halloween party.

07 The museum revealed it would be doing an exhibit on religious _____.

08 Marty and his son Bill have a _____ relationship. Things have always been strained between them.

09 I have no _____ attitude to challenging activities like base jumping or wing-suiting.

10 Convincing the jury was _____ to winning the case, but the crucial evidence was curiously "misplaced."

LESSON FORTY-SIX

B. Fill in the blanks in the passage with the most appropriate words.
Passage 46:

The urban planning conference thus far had been both _____ and dull. Lucy listened to long-winded lectures and _____ panels with little enthusiasm. Still, her new job had been a blessing. As a new employee, her relationship with the company was _____, and she knew it was crucial to her reputation that she stay alert and inquisitive during the conference. To do otherwise was _____ to career suicide. She was tasked with attending specific panels, interviewing different lecturers, and polling the attendees. Her boss had given Lucy only a _____ explanation of her duties to be completed at the conference. At first, she was daunted by the responsibility; the task made her very _____. Would she be fired if she didn't do well? She wished she had _____ abilities so she could read her boss's mind and see the standards he expected of her. During a Q & A on _____ agriculture, she felt herself falling asleep, despite her anxieties. The lecturer, a doctor from Harvard, read from his _____ of a dissertation, and it wasn't long before Lucy had fallen asleep completely. For the moment, her worries had been forgotten, and she enjoyed a dream in which she was eating a _____ dish of linguini alfredo.

LESSON FORTY-SEVEN

Target Words

1. Torrid
2. Tortuous
3. Tragedy
4. Tranquil
5. Travesty
6. Trek
7. Trite
8. Truculent
9. Ubiquitous
10. Ultimate

A. Fill in the blanks with the most appropriate words.

01 They aim to make their product _____ by promoting it internationally.

02 The _____ road to Hana is a dangerous but beautiful road that connects the town to Kahului.

03 It was a _____ of justice to deport the refugee family.

04 Lindsey felt embarrassed that her _____ affection for Parker was totally one-sided.

05 My dad and uncle _____ about the Himalayas when they were in their 30s.

06 The actor gave a _____ and very predictable acceptance speech at the Academy Awards last night.

07 My _____ fear is drowning, though I don't like cockroaches or heights either!

08 In his _____, abusive family, they settle things with their fists.

09 The biggest _____ of any war is the innocent people who get caught in the crossfire.

10 I have a sound machine that plays _____ white noise to help me sleep.

LESSON FORTY-SEVEN

B. Fill in the blanks in the passage with the most appropriate words.
Passage 47:

Many technophobes would agree that the _____ nature of current technology is a thing of concern. Some will engage in _____ arguments about the negative effects of iPhones, GPS, and virtual reality until they are red in the face. While some such arguments may be _____ and hard to follow, one discussion is taken far more seriously among skeptics and supporters alike: the existence of artificial intelligence, and what it means for the future. Once upon a time, a robot's ability to imitate humans was a _____ at best. Robots were clunky machines devoid of emotion, much less the capacity to mimic biological creatures. Now, the _____ concept of a "robot war" no longer feels so far-fetched. Even people like Stephen Hawking and Elon Musk have cautioned humans against advancing AI to the point of no return. Artificial intelligence has come a long way, and it still has quite a _____ ahead of it before it becomes any sort of imminent threat. For starters, robots cannot innately be _____ and destructive; they must be programmed to have such violent tendencies. The _____ goal of AI should not be to recreate humans, but to create a species that can help us make our world a better place to live in. Artificial intelligence was not created to be a workhorse. It would be a _____ to see such potential wasted on menial tasks. Humans could rest easy in the _____ notion of a future that sees humanity and artificial intelligence working together to accomplish more than either could accomplish on its own. Together, humans and robots could better the planet. But apart, they could destroy it.

LESSON FORTY-EIGHT

Target Words

1. Umbrage
2. Uncanny
3. Undulate
4. Uniform
5. Unilateral
6. Unique
7. Upbraid
8. Vacillate
9. Variance
10. Variegate

A. Fill in the blanks with the most appropriate words.

01 The nation finally agreed to _____ nuclear disarmament, providing that its enemy agree to a specified time of peace.

02 Her _____ was palpable. I could practically see the steam coming out of her ears.

03 It is _____ how some robots can perfectly mimic human movement and behaviour.

04 The teacher _____ Kevin for throwing food in class.

05 The ocean _____ for miles before it disappears over the horizon.

06 The way she appeared on social media was at _____ with the way she looked in real life.

07 I don't like to get between my friends when they fight. I always _____ between them and can never pick a side!

08 The soft, _____ colours in Monet's paintings are exquisite to behold both up close and from afar.

09 Small businesses are demanding that they receive _____ treatment from the banks.

10 Simone has a _____ approach to problem-solving. She will make a great engineer.

LESSON FORTY-EIGHT

B. Fill in the blanks in the passage with the most appropriate words.
Passage 48:

Harvey wanted to join the Air Force right out of high school. At first, his parents took _____ at the fact that Harvey might choose the military over a college education, but their _____ didn't last long. They saw how serious Harvey was about being in the Air Force, so after some _____, they finally sided with him and chose to support his decision. Harvey's father came around to the idea sooner than his mother, however. Harvey's father Ray explained to his wife Ester that their son would need the support of them both; _____ encouragement, from one parent or the other, was not enough. After some cajoling from both husband and son, Ester finally consented to Harvey's wishes. Harvey left on a Thursday. By Friday, he had been assigned a bunker and roommates. Harvey thought it was _____ how similar the bunker felt to a college dorm room. Soon, the _____ between college life and life in the Air Force would become much more evident. That night, they received what they were to wear during drills and training. Their sergeant made the rules _____ that they were allowed to wear plain clothes during class but still had to adhere to strict clothing guidelines. They were not allowed to wear graphic shirts or anything with crazy, _____ patterns and colours. Everything had to be either black, white, navy, or khaki. Harvey didn't mind the dress code. He had never had a _____ sense of style to begin with. As the days _____ into weeks, which turned into months, Harvey learned so much about himself and the Air Force. When he finally returned home for the holidays, Ray and Ester hardly recognized the man their boy had become!

LESSON FORTY-NINE

Target Words

1. Vast
2. Veneer
3. Veracious
4. Verbose
5. Vicarious
6. Vicissitudes
7. Vigour (US Vigor)
8. Vim
9. Vivacious
10. Vocation

A. Fill in the blanks with the most appropriate words.

01 Corinne is amazed by the amount of endurance and _____ it takes to run a full marathon.

02 The number of _____ I have had in the last three years alone is astounding!

03 After being diagnosed with ALS, Stephen Hawking pursued his _____ anyway.

04 My sister is going to Paris! I asked her to send me pictures so I could experience it _____ through her.

05 Even in his seventies he is still full of _____ and vigour.

06 Taylor's _____ sister is always the centre of every party.

07 The Italian orchard is _____ and beautiful. It extends over the horizon, into the sunset.

08 The motivational speaker is _____, but he has great comedic timing.

09 Though the witness swore to be _____, he was caught lying by the prosecuting lawyer.

10 Michael's _____ of impenetrable masculinity couldn't stand up to the stress of his new job.

LESSON FORTY-NINE

B. Fill in the blanks in the passage with the most appropriate words.
Passage 49:

Clem has always had a _____ personality. She likes to be the centre of attention, although no one would describe her as conceited. Rather, Clem is simply _____ and curious; she loves meeting new people and hearing their stories and, in turn, sharing her own. At first, Clem might appear to have the _____ of a meddlesome woman with too much _____, but her _____ can be attributed to the fact that she is actually quite an anxious person. In her adolescence, Clem would spend most of her time hiding away in her room. She would spend hours online, watching documentaries about _____ natural landscapes like the arctic tundra, the observable universe, and the deepest depths of the ocean. Soon, she moved onto documentaries that followed fascinating people who had faced countless _____ in their lives. Her favourite was a documentary called Man on Wire, about a hire-wire daredevil named Philippe Petit. Petit's _____ was high-wire artistry, meaning he would tightrope-walk between enormously tall skyscrapers, cathedrals, and bridges. Clem wanted to live _____ through Petit, whose bravery astounded her. Soon enough, however, Clem was inspired to step out of her comfort zone and start making friends. Ultimately, the _____ account of an adventurous tightrope walker had pushed her to be braver in her own life.

LESSON FIFTY

Target Words

1. Volition
2. Voluminous
3. Voluptuary
4. Wane
5. Wax
6. Weary
7. Weather
8. Whet
9. Winsome
10. Zeitgeist

A. Fill in the blanks with the most appropriate words.

01 The prince won't admit to being a _____, despite his massive mansion and numerous cars.

02 His anger _____ the longer he had to wait in line.

03 The lecturer _____ my interest when he mentioned ancient magic and alchemy.

04 Kel's desire to be a pro wrestler _____ after he graduated high school.

05 She broke the law of her own _____, and she'll have to pay the consequences!

06 A _____ smile slid across her face, and she laughed.

07 The Rolling Stones have a _____ discography.

08 The runner's feet and legs were _____ after running the marathon.

09 The boulders had been _____ away over time by the crashing waves.

10 Andy Warhol's work is a _____ of the 1960s US art scene.

LESSON FIFTY

B. Fill in the blanks in the passage with the most appropriate words.
Passage 50:

Frederick Douglass's 1845 autobiography, *Narrative of the Life of Frederick Douglass, an American Slave*, is a _____ book that depicts the _____ of an era in which slavery in America was still ubiquitous. Douglass was born into slavery in the state of Maryland. From a young age, Douglass knew his _____ was writing. When he was twelve, the plantation master's wife taught Frederick the alphabet. This knowledge _____ his appetite to learn more. After being harshly scolded by the plantation master for even learning the alphabet, Frederick started teaching himself to read and write in secret. As a result, his passion for writing _____. Many slave owners at the time were _____ white men with exorbitant demands. Douglass, however, only wanted to be a free man. Douglass attempted and failed to escape twice before he finally managed to escape successfully. It is testament to the man's willpower that he did not let his desire to be free _____ after two failed attempts. Douglass must have been _____ from being a slave for so long, but by 1838 he was finally a free man. He married a _____ free Black woman named Anna Murray, and together the two _____ many hardships throughout their lives. Still, they continued to fight for the abolition of slavery until Douglass's death in 1895.

www.ingramcontent.com/pod-product-compliance
Lightning Source LLC
Chambersburg PA
CBHW051255110526
44589CB00025B/2842